Student Mobility

Student Mobility

Creating an Environment for Social and Academic Success

Jane Stavem

ROWMAN & LITTLEFIELD
Lanham • Boulder • New York • London

Published by Rowman & Littlefield
A wholly owned subsidiary of The Rowman & Littlefield Publishing Group, Inc.
4501 Forbes Boulevard, Suite 200, Lanham, Maryland 20706
www.rowman.com

16 Carlisle Street, London W1D 3BT, United Kingdom

British Library Cataloguing in Publication Information Available

Library of Congress Cataloging-in-Publication Data

Stavem, Jane E.
Student mobility : creating an environment for social and academic success / Jane Stavem.
p. cm.
Includes bibliographical references.
ISBN 978-1-61048-976-8 (cloth : alk. paper) — ISBN 978-1-61048-977-5 (pbk.   ) —
ISBN 978-1-61048-978-2 (electronic) 1. Student mobility—United States. 2. Academic achieve-
ment—United States. I. Title.
LA230.S745 2014
371.2'91—dc23

2013045781

Printed in the United States of America

This book is dedicated to Jody.
Thank you for telling me I write well.

Contents

Acknowledgments

The journey of a career travels through many places, but it is the faces along the way that make the difference. So many faces have influenced me, each of them making me a better educator and a better person.

But there are some people that play a unique role in shaping your future picture of yourself, and I would like to recognize them because they truly kept me on the path of education from the very early days of my life.

My parents have always been encouragers and at an early age told me I could be a teacher. I had an old desk in the basement where I could play school and begin forming my vision of teaching students in my very own classroom.

In elementary school, I had wonderful teachers. My second grade teacher, Mrs. James, allowed me to read to the class from the tall blue chair. My fourth grade teacher, Mrs. Fredrickson, let me have old teacher's manuals and textbooks when they were ready to be discarded. I felt like I had the keys to the kingdom! My sixth grade teacher, Miss Hollins, taught me about having fun in a classroom and using your creativity to make learning exciting.

In high school, Dr. Sharp helped me believe I could do whatever I set out to do, and challenged me to do more than I thought I could.

In college, I learned from Dr. Nancy Vall and Dr. Gloria Kortmeyer and saw the first great examples of female administrators. At that point I set my sights on becoming a principal someday.

After I started teaching, Dr. Bill Schrankler nudged me to begin my administrative program and began mentoring me to become a building leader.

And finally, at a critical point in my career, I was encouraged to begin my doctoral program by leaders at the University of Nebraska and began looking at district leadership as a possibility.

So now I find myself well down the path of education and can trace many of the influences that brought me to this wonderful profession and kept me traveling down the road. I am so thankful for just the right people at just the right time, and I look forward to meeting new people on the path I have yet to travel.

Most of all, I am thankful and deeply indebted to my family for walking with me down the path of long hours, maximum school events, and little anonymity.

To my husband, who always makes sure I have my coffee and my bag in the car each morning and a quiet place to work, I thank you for all of your sacrifices that allow me to do what I love.

To my children, who often put up with a mother that came home late and left early, I thank you for understanding the professional calling on my life. You have always known you come first, but knew many other children were also very important.

Thank you to all who have been on the path, for the journey is far more important than the destination.

Foreword

Cassandra Erkens

To say "times are changing" would be an understatement in education. There are so many glaringly obvious changes capturing the attention of today's educators: teaching for twenty-first century skills, integrating technology, incorporating new standards, ensuring all learners will be career and college ready, aligning instruction to support global jobs that haven't even been created yet, engaging and retaining the younger, "millennial" staff, and moving from isolation to collaboration in our day to day work, to name just a few. It would be easy to get lost in the dazzling appeal and urgent need of some of these changes and thereby miss some of the profound changes that are more subtle, but equally significant.

In this book, author Jane Stavem outlines one such subtle but profound change that is already impacting schools at an alarming but discounted pace: the mobility rate of today's learners is increasing and the needs of the learners trapped in these situations are as demanding as they have ever been. As Dr. Stavem points out, the increase is troubling: school change hinders the social, emotional, and academic development of *each* learner and frequent changes in schools makes it virtually impossible for traditional schools to address those significant, growing concerns.

Mobile learners are at risk for remaining illiterate in math, reading, and writing skills. The social and economic costs of illiteracy are staggeringly high. Today there are many available reports from various organizations that highlight the powerful, negative global impact of illiteracy: Limited employability; perpetual poverty; lost business opportunities, productivity, and wealth creation; compromised health; increased crime; expanded welfare needs; eroding family and social structures; and the list could continue. It goes without saying that the tax on illiteracy is a cost that *everyone* pays. Repeatedly.

And educators are at risk when mobility rates are rising and support systems are minimal and insufficient. In a culture of high accountability, with no leniency granted to factors outside of a school's control (for example, a student moved in to the school the day before the high stakes exams were given), the problems that emerge capture national headlines: schools are reconstituted, jobs are lost, funding is withdrawn, and educators engage in questionable ethics. The costs to *everyone*—educators, their learners, families, and society at large—are staggering when educational institutions ignore the silent but lethal conundrum of increasing mobility rates.

Yet, in all of our school improvement plans, little attention has been paid to mobility rates. Frankly, the problem has not been on our educational radar for a variety of reasons: 1) it lacks luster compared to discussions of global demands and twenty-first century skills; 2) the impact on the learners and their families is obscured by their already marginalized voices; and 3) the epidemic has been growing silently but steadily and it is only beginning to reach the critical mass required to capture the attention of national policy makers.

Fortunately, with this book Dr. Stavem puts the issue squarely on our radar *and* creates the obligation for schools to address it. She notes, "It does not really matter if the mobility rate is 98 percent or 5 percent; every child and family that walks through the front doors of a school matters." She responds with compassion, wisdom, authority, and practicality, as she takes the readers on a pathway that provides a comprehensive response to increasing mobility rates in schools:

- Chapters 1–3 outline and define the many issues involved in student mobility.
- Chapter 4 provides an overview of the features that schools must consider and address in their systematic approach to mobile learners.
- Chapters 5–12 offer the provocative questions and critical ideas schools should reflect upon as they strive to accommodate their students in transition—from invitation to closure in a school relationship and from the classroom to the community at large.
- Chapter 13 provides specific and practical examples through a case study approach with voices from the field showcasing possibilities for successful responses.
- Chapter 14 delves into the legal ramifications and considerations for schools committing to this journey.
- Chapter 15 sounds the clarion call that compels schools to take action and address the needs of mobile learners and the educators who serve them.

Finally, the appendices present the questions and tools offered inside the book as a separate list to support anyone interested in addressing this critical work, the scenarios to support reflective conversations and decision making for staff engaged in the process, as well as sample action plans. This book provides a wealth of resources to support schools in addressing a complex problem.

As Dr. Stavem states, "Children deserve the best a school has to offer from the moment they walk in the door to the time they walk out." She continues by asserting that our educational responses to children who are not in control of the movement of their families can *never* be less than adequate. Throughout history, we have far too many examples of society providing insurmountable obstacles to the downtrodden because of ignorance regarding their circumstances and experiences.

The voices of the marginalized are rarely heard, giving those who are not marginalized little reason to attend. In this book, Dr. Stavem gives voice to marginalized mobile learners and requires us to attend. If the purpose of education is to prepare our learners to be successful in life, and we have the moral obligation to prepare *all* of our learners, then we must attend to the demanding needs of our mobile learners. We must tackle the complex issues involved so we can get about the business of truly educating *each* of our learners.

Preface

As a new principal, I began dreading the days when new families would walk into our school office to enroll their children because it meant I was going to have to deliver the news that some teacher was going to get a new student in the classroom. Many teachers welcomed them with open arms, but some were less than thrilled.

We would go through a process of reviewing class lists, remembering which teacher had taken the last new student and looking at the general makeup of each list.

I would make the decision; then my secretary and I would play rock, paper, scissors to see which of us would break the news, enduring the subtle sighing, rolling of eyes, and general disgust at the inconvenience that was created as a result of the arrival.

Then we would walk away, hoping the incoming student would not have to endure the wrath of a situation that was certainly outside the control of a child.

If the counselor was at our school, she would gladly help orient the student to the building and provide a familiar face throughout the first day. But she was there only two days a week so that was never a guaranteed solution.

Some classrooms had wonderful practices in place to help new students, but others adopted the "sink or swim" immersion model, leaving students feeling disconnected at best and downright unwanted at worst.

If the family came in during lunch, few people were available to assist them due to supervision schedules and planning times. If a child was in the nurse's office, or the secretary was assisting a teacher in the back room on the copy machine, no one may have even see them come into the office for a few minutes, so a parent may have stood at the counter wondering if anyone was going to help them.

As a school, we knew our systems were not in place, so we began to address the problem by implementing some new practices in the office so we could standardize our level of care for families when they came to enroll children.

At about the same time, we became a Schoolwide Title I school and knew one component of the rubric by which we would be evaluated required us to have a transition plan in place to meet the needs of our mobile students.

These additional measures were somewhat helpful, but it still was not enough. Ultimately, we knew we needed to do a better job for the students and families who came through our front doors no matter what time of year it was and no matter how many times they had changed schools.

We needed a change in plans and attitudes so that everyone throughout the school knew what was expected, and no matter what classroom received a new student, the quality of the transition would be the best we could provide.

The process of developing a solid transition plan should not be left to chance for any school, and my experiences within multiple schools have shown me that people want to do a good job, they just may not have all the right tools in place to do so.

Even when we know the negative effects of student mobility, we are not always moved to action. Schools may have tried to put practices in place here and there, but have not fully engaged in a solid process that results in a clear plan with consistent practices that can be followed with any measure of fidelity.

Building leaders must provide the focus and the framework that allow staff members to collectively develop a plan of action. Whether you are part of a high school, a middle school, or an elementary school, students need to have effective transitions in order to be successful socially and academically. Plans can be developed at all levels to ensure practices are consistently followed every time a new student is enrolled.

It would be easy to copy the plan of another school and put a new name at the top, but it is the process that allows the practices to be internalized as discussions about the real needs of students and families ensue with those who will develop and follow the plan. The value of this process cannot be overstated.

In the process of developing a plan, other attitudes and perceptions about issues related to student and family diversity may emerge. This provides another opportunity for people to move to a deeper level in their ability to understand and meet the needs of all students who come to enroll.

This is a process that should not be rushed but also not delayed. Whether you use this resource at the beginning of a year, during the year, or at the end of a year, anytime is the right time to plan for the social and academic success of all students in your care.

If your school is suffering from the effects of the revolving door with no plan for transitions, it is time to commit to a better way of serving mobile students.

Introduction

A Familiar Scene

Every day it is becoming a more familiar scene in schools across the country. A new family arrives in the school office to enroll children, but it is not the beginning of the school year. It is not the first time the children have changed schools, and it is not even the first time they have changed schools during that year.

In fact, it may be a change in enrollment that falls within a long line-up of school changes, all through no fault of the child. Yet it is the children who are left to deal with the effects of school change as it impacts their social, emotional, and academic growth and development.

Too often this scenario falls into a succession of similar situations for many families and the schools where they arrive. It may be a string of different families or the same families making a series of repetitive moves.

The cumulative effect from multiple moves can be a growing sense of frustration and apathy on the part of both the families and the schools. Families are under the continuing stress of situations that have led to frequent moves, and schools feel the strain of continuous disruption and interruption of schedules and services.

MOBILITY HAPPENS

The number of students who move in and out of schools fluctuates on a day-to-day, month-to-month, and year-to-year basis, and the cause of those statistics are largely beyond our control.

A school with relatively low mobility may have a number of changes within a short amount of time, and the effects of those moves have a heavy impact, given the typical rate of change.

By contrast, a school with very high mobility may have the same number of changes within a short amount of time but feel relatively unaffected due to the normal frequency of change.

In either scenario, the changes are relative to the setting and the actual mobility statistic is irrelevant. Whether schools experience low mobility or high mobility, students still come and go at all times during the school year because of multiple factors.

1

When we think about the presence or absence of a formal mobility plan, there may be a tendency to use statistics to justify the presence or absence of solid practices.

When schools have moderate to high levels of mobility, the need is more apparent because of the frequency of student and family transitions. Mobility becomes more noticeable and is seen as a common part of the school culture, or the norm of the environment.

Schools with high mobility are viewed to have more need due to that frequency, but schools with lower mobility may not have the same sense of urgency and therefore, do not see it as an issue that needs to be addressed.

MANAGING MOBILITY

When schools encounter the effects of frequent mobility, it is common to seek ways to control it, looking for strategies that help students maintain some level of stability.

The fact of the matter is that in reality, schools can do very little to control the factors that contribute to student mobility. Schools cannot control rent, job gain or loss, divorce, mental health, military deployment, addiction, or eviction.

NAMES NOT NUMBERS

A lot of studies and reports focus on the statistics and causes of mobility. Much attention has been given to that data, yet very few resources address the practical side of dealing with the reality of mobility. The few that do largely fail to provide an actual process for establishing plans and processes at a school level.

This book purposefully does not focus on the numbers tied to mobility because in terms of practice, the frequency of mobile students does not matter. It is time to pay more attention to names rather than numbers.

Whether there are two new students in a given year or two hundred, the practices used to help those students transition into a new environment should be purposeful and planned. Whether the district or school mobility rate is 10 percent or 80 percent, students must be viewed as individuals when entering a new school.

WHERE WE START

Knowing we have little control over the endless revolving door for students who come and go from school to school, including causes for the moves, we have to begin focusing on the things we can control.

What can be controlled are the processes schools use to manage student mobility over time, to provide consistency and quality of services to students and families. No matter how many times a family walks through the school door to enroll or uproot a child, schools can support the movement with solid systems that are followed with fidelity.

MORE THAN FORMS

Many schools mistakenly think they already have these systems in place by virtue of the stack of forms that are required for the enrollment process. Supported moves for mobile students require more than just forms, more than even distribution of students on class lists, and more than a brief introduction at the door of a new classroom.

It requires more than one person doing things the right way, and doing things the right way more than once. It requires the commitment of an entire school to move past wanting to control the factors that cause mobility and making the shift to controlling the strategies that support mobility.

ESSENTIAL COMPONENTS — DISTRICT LEADERSHIP

District leaders play a critical role in ensuring effective practices are applied in a coherent and cohesive manner. Superintendents in districts large and small are catalysts for effective systems that permeate all schools.

In larger districts, there are often multiple schools with varying demographics. It is up to the superintendent to see that all schools account for mobile students, as they move within and without the district.

Successful transition processes begin and end with administrative leadership that assumes responsibility for all students. There is no question that procedures can be mandated to address the needs of mobile students.

When leaders are willing to guide staff members through a process that collectively identifies a need and develops authentic, shared leadership, the possibility of lasting change is far more likely. Entire districts are able to collectively share in the responsibility for helping students and families in the transition process.

ESSENTIAL COMPONENTS — BUILDING LEADERSHIP

Building principals directly influence the climate and culture and are responsible for multiple practices within a school. They are the ones who provide vital leadership for an entire community of staff members, and set the tone for how mobile students will be treated as they enter and exit their school.

In order for them to do this well, there has to be a plan, and it is up to the principal to see that one is developed and implemented over time by working through an effective process with those who will ultimately carry it out.

ESSENTIAL COMPONENTS—ADMINISTRATIVE LEADERSHIP

In addition to district leadership, superintendents play a critical role in educating the Board of Education on the effects of student mobility. In order to facilitate systemic changes to support mobility, district policies must align with district practices to support positive outcomes.

School board members are directly responsible for ensuring policies are in place, and rely on the superintendent to provide not only statistical information on mobility, but also information specific to schools, areas within a community, and specific issues that arise from student and family mobility.

They are representatives of the community and are responsible for connecting the needs of the district with the resources and support of the community. They can also shape community perceptions in order to focus on opportunities rather than excuses.

ESSENTIAL COMPONENTS—FISCAL COMMITMENT

District budgets play an important role in the big picture of supporting student mobility. District resources must be aligned with district needs which must include the practices that support mobility, including adequate staffing, transportation, before and after school programs, and parent education.

When a budget is brought before a Board of Education for approval, ultimately there must be agreement that the needs of the district are being met with the allocation of funds. If budgets are not adequate, schools are limited in their ability to support students and families.

ESSENTIAL COMPONENTS—DISTRICT VISION AND PURPOSE

Regardless of district size, there must be a collective sense of ownership at a central level for the success of mobile students.

In larger districts there may be resources in place to support mobile students from many different angles. There may be district personnel hired specifically to monitor things such as the homeless student population, immigrant family arrivals, and transitional needs for students who have been placed within correctional facilities.

In smaller districts, the central supports may be more limited in scope and may be connected to personnel such as transportation directors, food service staff, student services, and the office of the superintendent.

It is imperative that all districts, large and small, understand that mobile students exist everywhere. Some of the needs are very similar from place to place, while others are very different depending on the location and school district.

District office personnel, superintendents, and Boards of Education must be ready to step up and support their schools as they develop essential practices to support all mobile students. They must understand the needs, allocate resources effectively, and expect that all students will be treated with the care and respect they deserve no matter how many times they transition in or out of a school in that district.

WHY YOU NEED THIS BOOK

This book views the people who work at the school level as the experts in knowing and understanding their unique student populations.

The purpose of this book is to provide a process that allows essential leaders to guide their schools through a series of questions that result in solid systems designed to support student mobility.

It offers a simple process to help schools assess current realities, provide concrete steps to recognize areas of strength, and strengthen areas of weakness.

WALKING THROUGH THE PROCESS—GETTING STARTED

Chapters 1 through 4 are designed to bring context to the subject of mobility as staff members begin thinking about their own attitudes toward mobile students. These chapters can be used to begin conversations and spark thinking as realities of a specific school are considered.

There may be a variety of attitudes and opinions surrounding the issue of student mobility and, before an entire school can effectively meet the needs of mobile students, those issues need to be identified, addressed, and discussed in order for everyone to ultimately feel a sense of ownership in what is developed.

CONTINUING THE PROCESS—DEVELOPING A PLAN

As the book progresses, the ideas and questions contained in chapters 5 through 12 are designed to walk school leaders and staff members through a process that can be adapted to any level, leading to the development of action steps that are appropriate for your school.

In doing so, you will arrive at solutions grounded in best practice and customized for your unique population and community of learners.

KEEPING IT REAL—VOICES FROM THE FIELD

Chapters 13 through 15 and the appendixes offer a reality check as voices are heard from those who are implementing effective practices. Information is offered on related issues that arise, directly affecting the complexities of some situations accompanying mobile students, making some scenarios very difficult for school personnel.

THE END GOAL—PRACTICES MEET PLAN

The most important outcome of using this book is the development of a real plan that serves as a consistent guide for effective practices which can be reviewed and modified over time as needed.

The plan leads to consistency in using best practices that can be shared from school to school and district to district.

It leads to more effective communication within groups and between groups of people throughout a district.

It allows a network of expertise to grow and connect to strengthen systems that support students and families.

The process and resulting mobility plan serve as the bedrock for all other initiatives that schools put in place to support student achievement. Academic, social, and emotional interventions and supports are far more likely to be successful if mobile students are supported in the transition process.

When students and families are immediately connected, all other efforts can be maximized in terms of effectiveness. Schools and districts become more purposeful by eliminating wasted time, money, and effort. Most importantly, there is a much higher probability for mobile students to realize high achievement and hope for successful graduation.

GETTING IT RIGHT—GETTING STARTED

It is true that the forces requiring families to make frequent moves between schools are difficult to control, but it is time for schools to begin taking steps to assure that no matter how often a family walks through the school doors to enroll a child, the same practices should be in place whether it is at the beginning of the year, the middle of the year, or almost the end of the year.

Children deserve the best a school has to offer from the moment they walk in the door to the time they walk out. Children are not in control of the movement of their families, and the welcome they often receive when coming to a new school is less than adequate.

This book does not supply all of the answers for how schools should plan for effective transitions for mobile students, but rather asks the right questions. Every school and district is faced with unique needs related to student mobility.

Plans should reflect those needs in the specific actions laid out to assure successful transitions for all students. Ideas will be offered, but the value of this book is the process that allows a staff to collectively arrive at a shared sense of purpose in planning and carrying out a vision for helping mobile students.

The power of systematic practices will impact the academic and social success of every student, no matter how long they stay in one location.

ONE

Mobility in Context

Painting the Picture

Student mobility has long been seen as a problem removed from rural areas and communities with seemingly stable populations. However, data indicate that a high percentage of student mobility is now found in many settings, including small towns as well as in the urban setting. Student mobility factors arise from a variety of issues, ranging from socioeconomic constraints to migrant employment for families.

The result for a highly mobile student is that he or she may enter school at varying points throughout the school year, from the first week right up to the last days of school. The educational impact of a highly mobile population affects the incoming student as well as the students in the existing classroom receiving the new student.

In the current age of accountability, it has never been more critical to identify and replicate effective practices as a way of addressing some of the most critical needs of highly mobile students.

It is also necessary to have a solid understanding of the factors that led to the practices which have been effectively implemented in schools in order to make connections between the primary causes of student mobility and what works. Once these two factors are identified, schools can begin to gain support for sustainable practices that result in successful transitions for highly mobile students.

Most importantly, theoretical information regarding both causes and practices can translate directly into action.

Student mobility has become an issue that is connected with a number of different accountability areas within education. Two of the most common are Title I and migrant education.

TITLE I AND MOBILITY

For schools that have been categorized as Schoolwide Title I programs, effective transition practices become part of the required plan of action. A Schoolwide program permits a school to use funds from Title I, Part A and other federal education program funds and resources to upgrade the entire educational program of the school in order to raise academic achievement for all the students.

Opportunities provided by these types of programs are designed to assist schools, districts, and states in raising the achievement level of all children, but particularly those who have always been the intended beneficiaries of Title I—poor children, low-achieving children, migrant children, children who are neglected or at risk of dropping out, and limited-English-proficient children.

Title I requires a focus on a results-based accountability approach for reinforcing this commitment. This approach is designed to provide the public with information on how schools and districts are doing in raising the achievement of different groups of students.

A comprehensive plan, required for Schoolwide Title I schools, must be developed within a one-year period of a school obtaining Schoolwide status. Comprehensive plans must address the needs of all children in the school, but particularly the needs of children who are members of the target population of any federal education program whose funds are included in the Schoolwide program.

A rubric is used in the review process to determine if all required components are in place. Part of the rubric focuses on a required transition plan and indicates practices must be put in place to help mobile students transition between grade levels and between buildings. Things such as effective orientation practices for students and families are to be included with an eye on specific cultural needs or accommodations that should be considered.

The rubric indicates that student mobility is an issue that impacts the overall academic achievement and social-emotional adjustment for students in Title I schools. It can be assumed that the educational programs of all schools are impacted by student mobility, and because of the degree of impact, the expectation exists for specific practices to be implemented to address the needs of mobile students.

FEDERAL PROGRAM INFLUENCE

Title I is the largest federal program in K–12 education. It has evolved over the past thirty years into its present form, allowing schools with the required percentage of poor children to use those funds to upgrade an entire school in order to raise the academic achievement levels of all children.

This regulatory change that allows flexible use of Title I funds, as opposed to targeting only qualifying students for academic assistance, reduced the fragmentation of programs and allowed schools to integrate services based on both the needs of the Title I students and other students within the building.

The number of Title I schools eligible to run a Schoolwide program has increased significantly over the past ten years due to changes in eligibility factors as well as rising numbers of disadvantaged students in some school districts.

The intent of Schoolwide Title I funding was to ensure the involvement of parents, community members, teachers, and administrators in the decision-making processes of the school, while maximizing funding and program options to improve student learning. School improvement plans were a central component that guided the efforts and initiatives designed to raise student achievement.

Accountability factors are present in yearly reviews of the improvement plans, which are measured against the Title I Peer Review Rubric. Feedback is provided from state Title I representatives and ongoing progress must be documented and reported.

Schoolwide Title I programs are supported by research that indicates all academic performance can be negatively affected when high levels of poverty are present. For students to meet high standards, all instructional programs must be supported, not just those addressing the needs of lower performing students.

Teachers in successful schools have high expectations for all students, and when an entire school is implementing change initiatives, even the most disadvantaged students can achieve.

MOBILITY DEFINED

Because Schoolwide eligibility is based on the percentage of disadvantaged students, it can also be said that students from this same group may experience a higher rate of mobility than students from higher socioeconomic groups. Student mobility is defined as movement in or out of a given school during the course of the school year.

There is a large body of research that supports the negative impact of high mobility on student achievement, with a variety of causative factors. While work is being done to ensure the quality of instructional programs is well in place, some of the accompanying symptoms of the qualifying groups may be overlooked when schools are planning effective programs to meet the academic needs of students in Schoolwide Title I schools.

Reading and math programs are overhauled, additional personnel may be hired, and new instructional practices may be implemented. However, what is often overlooked are the practices and procedures that need to be in place to help highly mobile students make the initial transitions into school successfully and for the instructional interventions to be received once they begin school.

Little research is available in terms of the relationship between rates of student mobility and procedures that are put in place to address those specific needs in order to provide for a child's academic, social, and emotional needs as they make the transition to a new school.

Guidelines exist for best practices in helping schools assimilate mobile students into a new school. However, a strong connection does not necessarily exist between high numbers of mobile students and the number and type of specific components that should be in place.

There are schools that have realized the needs of mobile students and as a result, have made specific changes to accommodate the needs. It is critical to identify these schools and examine the practices that have been implemented in order to replicate what works.

MIGRANT VERSUS MOBILE

An assumption is often made that highly mobile students are the same as migrant students. Migrant students are defined as those students whose parent/guardian is a migratory fisher, dairy worker, or agricultural worker, and who have moved from one school district to another in the preceding thirty-six months for a parent to obtain temporary or seasonal employment in agricultural or fishing work.

In certain locations, migrant students account for a large part of the mobile student population, but this does not hold true for all areas. Other causes of mobility can be linked to military families, socioeconomic constraints and poverty, and changes in family structure due to death, divorce, incarceration, or blended families.

BARRIERS

While many schools have larger populations of highly mobile students, effective practices are not necessarily put into place even when it is evident that the need exists to do so. Mitigating factors may be finances, lack of personnel, lack of adequate knowledge to implement effective measures, or inability to initiate changes to meet the needs of students.

Other prohibitive factors may include an unwillingness to implement procedures and practices to meet the needs of highly mobile students based on racial prejudice, denial of the problem, or the belief that such procedures are meaningless because students are not present long enough to benefit and will simply move to another school.

ACADEMIC AND SOCIAL DISRUPTION

Highly mobile students move in and out of schools multiple times throughout the year, often within the same district. Each time students move, their odds for success are statistically diminished. They are forced to establish new peer groups and significant relationships. They are introduced to a new curriculum, and while state academic standards somewhat address the issue of what is taught at a particular grade level, they do not necessarily determine the timeframe in which the content is taught.

Therefore, students often miss chunks of information and may be at risk academically because of the differences in district curriculum and instructional pacing.

Classrooms also experience a period of adjustment each time a student enters or leaves the classroom. New students may distract existing classrooms if there is disruption in existing social structures and an impact on established peer relationships. In other words, the pecking order must be reestablished.

While this affects students, it also impacts the classroom teacher as negative behaviors erupt, disruptions occur, and students who may have been doing well begin to display new negative behaviors. Academic disruption occurs when student needs do not align with the current instructional concepts, and as a result, individualized planning must occur.

MISSING INFORMATION

As parents contemplate additional school moves, schools with high levels of mobility must address the element of parental education. Parents need to understand the impact of mobility on academic success and failure. In order to accomplish this there are numerous procedures and practices that can be implemented to ease the process of coming to a new school as well as leaving it.

This book seeks to raise the awareness and proficiency of all school personnel by identifying practices that are currently meeting the needs of mobile populations and making connections between what can be done with what is being done in effective schools.

It is imperative that students are met with open arms when they come, and sent out with fond farewells when they leave in order to help them achieve as much as they can during the time they are enrolled in any school. It is equally imperative that schools move from ideas and suggestions to action, with plans designed for consistent implementation over time.

Whether the setting is an elementary, middle, or high school, promising practices can be implemented to enhance the transition process whether it is part of a mandate or just part of best practice.

ESSENTIAL IDEAS

- Student mobility is a complex issue. It is an issue that continues to impact classrooms and schools, so much so that it continues to be discussed and researched in hopes of knowing how best to deal with the outcomes and mitigate the causes.
- In reality there are no solutions to stop mobility. Solutions imply there are ways to fix something and keep it resolved over time. This has never been and will never be the case with student mobility.
- We can successfully manage the dilemma of student mobility by moving past knowing what research and statistics say to dealing with it by taking appropriate action.

TWO

Reality of the Revolving Door

Attitudes and Perceptions

Picture the following scenario: It is the day before the high-stakes student achievement tests are set to begin. The principal appears at the fourth grade doorway and announces that the school is getting two new students the next day.

The teacher proceeds to ask if the new students have to take the test since they just arrived at the school. The principal knows the requirement is to include the students, with the collective assumption that the outcome will negatively affect overall school performance.

After reviewing the limited cumulative files for the incoming students, it is clear that achievement is already well below grade level, and there are significant gaps in learning. The learning is not reflective of the incoming school, yet the achievement will be counted as if it were.

It is a familiar scene in schools all across our nation. The front door opens, and a family appears in the office ready to enroll new students into existing classrooms. Unfortunately, the other factors that often accompany this scenario are also becoming increasingly common.

What was once thought of as a typical first day of school now happens at virtually any point throughout the school year. Students may arrive with or without supplies ready to begin the day in their new classrooms. Parents may or may not have adequate records and information to complete the enrollment process.

Students may be entering their first new school or their next new school in a long succession of schools, knowing this arrangement may be temporary at best. Parents may enroll their children at a logical point in the year that serves as a natural transition point, such as following a break in the calendar year, or at the end of a quarter or semester.

15

But some parents are completely unaware that such times would be better for their children to make the transition, and enroll them according to their schedule that follows an eviction notice, the divorce decree, or the location of the next significant other who has come into the family picture.

TIMING IS EVERYTHING

The transition may not follow the neatly composed schedule of the school calendar for the purposes of high-stakes testing, semester exams, or the beginning of the next chapter or unit in the textbook. In short, what was once a typical event at the beginning of the school year is now a daily event that is neither neat nor convenient for either the family and students or the receiving school district. It is often uncomfortable, time-consuming, and confusing.

Research has produced abundant evidence about the causes and effects of mobility. But the moment a family arrives at a school to enroll children, all of the research in the educational world is irrelevant unless it has been translated into appropriate action leading to the right conditions being in place for student success.

GAPS AND SPACES

Unfortunately, even though educators may be aware of the conditions necessary for success, a new student may still be faced with feeling cold shoulders from teachers, confusion with learning new classroom and school routines, and somehow the blame is placed squarely on their very small shoulders.

Students may be placed in classrooms based on the teacher that got the last new student, where an empty desk exists, or where there is an unused nametag that still matches the original classroom set. The gaps in learning may go unnoticed, and if discovered, are quickly buried or ignored in order to avoid inconvenient review sessions or individualized skill instruction.

WELCOME TO OUR SCHOOL

As families come to a new school, there may be a variety of perceptions that result from the first visit. Parents may be made to feel they are a huge inconvenience in a very busy office, or perceive their need for language translation is less than appreciated. They may be asked to complete a mountain of papers that require documents they left behind, either packed in boxes or that simply no longer exist.

They may leave with a feeling of disconnection at best and complete confusion and distrust at worst. If the need arises to come to school after the point of enrollment, parents may hesitate to risk such an encounter for fear of a repeat performance and may ask students to undertake parental responsibilities rather than face the music themselves.

SPECIAL NEEDS

Behavioral needs, special accommodations, and medical issues can increase the complexity and confusion of the enrollment process. Often, the best hope in the back of school personnel's minds may be that the transitory pattern of the student will continue, and existing mobility statistics will take him right out the very door he just came in if the teacher can hold out long enough.

The student and his family will then become the problem of the next location, and the cycle is repeated with fractured fragments of learning being pieced together like a mismatched puzzle.

The unluckiest recipient is the school and district that will be forced to report the achievement results of the mobile student as part of their local and state assessment requirements. Scores that could once be eliminated from spreadsheets, or delayed until testing was completed, must now be counted wherever and whenever the student is enrolled at the point of testing.

A BETTER OPTION

What if the best hope was not to count on mobile students leaving again? What if the best hope rested on the consistent use of strategies that work, allowing every new student the opportunity for success the moment he arrived? What if schools developed simple systems for receiving mobile students and believed that those systems were part of the fundamental values of the school and the district? And what if every student and every family had the same quality experience every time they entered a new school, no matter what time of the year they chose or were forced to make a move?

No longer would the process be left to chance or to the mood of the day in the school office. No longer would students be at greater risk for failure because of the lack of information for their new teacher. No longer would teachers see new students as an inconvenience or an element of fairness doled out to them from the administration.

The fact of the matter is that regardless of how well we understand student mobility and all of the related factors, regardless of how many times we have new students enter our schools, and regardless of how we would like to make it stop, new students will keep coming.

For some schools this happens as a daily occurrence. For other schools it is once in a blue moon, and the rest fall somewhere in between for the frequency of student mobility.

EVERY CHILD MATTERS

It does not really matter if the mobility rate is 98 percent or 5 percent; every child and every family that walks through the front doors of a school matters. We may not like the reasons that brought them and may not like having to keep them with all of the baggage that is part of the package, but why risk making an inevitable situation worse when steps can be taken to actively improve the process?

Why not take situations that are potentially positive in isolation, and replicate them for more students over time?

ESSENTIAL IDEAS

- Schools have to accept the fact that student mobility is a reality and deal with it head on.
- Let's shed the negative coat that shrouds the effects of mobility and replace it with a cloak of optimism and empowerment that blankets an entire school and spreads throughout a district.
- Let's apply what we know and do our best for every student, every time, in every school.

THREE

Mobility and the Poverty Factor

One of the resulting effects of poverty that has been well documented is a high rate of student mobility, or the rate at which students frequently change schools. Student mobility refers to changes in school enrollment at times other than those prompted by school or program design.

While many studies focus on the link between mobility and decreased academic achievement, this aspect is difficult to prove, given the multiple factors that occur when a student changes schools. Mobility may be only a symptom rather than a cause of poor school performance.

There are also significant differences in voluntary and involuntary moves. Voluntary movement for students and families may result from financial and career success within families, while those who move involuntarily may be compelled to do so because of economic difficulties or family disruptions such as divorce or abuse.

SUPPORTED AND UNSUPPORTED MOVES

There are also differences between supported and unsupported moves. Supported moves usually involve time to plan ahead, tour a school, and make a choice for when and how the move will take place. The adults in charge understand the impact on the child and can take steps to help them think through and deal with the resulting transition.

An unsupported move involves little adult understanding or skill in helping the child to deal with the transition, and depends more fully on the school to assume the role of transition specialist. There may be a distinct absence of involvement due to whatever the adult may be dealing with. They may simply be in survival mode and do not have the capacity to do much more than get themselves and their family to another location.

19

After the move, they either deal with the aftermath, or deny it. Adults may understand the implications but are still left with no choice. They may even glamorize the move, focusing on the aspect of a "fresh start" to help the children cope.

RURAL VERSUS URBAN MOBILITY

Historically, student mobility has often been viewed as a problem exclusive to urban areas. However, rural counterparts are beginning to see the rise in mobility as well. Residential moves and school transfers are higher in the United States than in any other industrialized country. It is also believed, through multiple studies, that mobility diminishes the likelihood of graduation.

Students have a higher probability of dropping out due to the cumulative effect of instructional gaps from frequent school changes, high rates of absenteeism, and low self-esteem because of fewer lasting peer connections. Students who attend the same school for their entire career are most likely to graduate.

PERCEPTIONS OF MOBILITY—A BROADER VIEW

While mobility affects students and student achievement, there are also very real effects on the schools that receive and send mobile students. These effects can be categorized into the areas of teacher views, curriculum, staff morale, student records, testing, social effects, and parent views.

TEACHER VIEWS

Teachers often equate student mobility with extra work. Teachers must take time to help acclimate new students, find out their level of instruction, help them to fit in and make friends, and learn the rules and routines of the classroom and school. If a teacher initially expects less of a student as a result of starting from behind, the lower expectations may result in negative reactions and a reluctance to establish a positive relationship with the child, all resulting in lower achievement.

If a student is significantly ahead of peers, additional time may also be required for individualized planning, project development, and all with the risk of the student leaving after much time and effort are expended generating appropriate accommodations.

CURRICULUM AND ACADEMIC NEED—WHERE TO START

When mobile students arrive in the classroom it is always necessary to assess the child's present skill level to determine where they need to progress academically. However, this is often problematic due to ineffective record transfer procedures.

A teacher may have to put some things on hold for stable students in order to spend time with the new arrival. It also may mean the teacher continues working with existing students, and a paraeducator is assigned the task of working on remedial or advanced work.

This means the person with the most expertise in instruction may not be working with the student who has the highest academic need. If there is no concrete plan, a teacher may simply attempt to make progress where she can and move the student on to the next grade regardless of actual achievement.

STAFF MORALE—STRESS OVER TIME

Schools with high rates of mobility can be extremely demanding places to teach for experienced and inexperienced teachers alike, and they are often staffed by new or less experienced teachers.

In high mobility schools, teacher mobility itself may be a contributor to the overall instability of the school almost as much as the rate of student mobility. Therefore, it is imperative that staff members realize the impact of student mobility and work to minimize its effects on both fronts.

TRANSFER OF STUDENT RECORDS AND ASSESSMENT DATA

The exchange of student records between districts and schools is often problematic due to delays and inefficient systems. Some records are held in an attempt to collect fees or late payments. Others are difficult to obtain because school offices are understaffed and unable to process the paperwork in a timely manner.

Records may be transferred digitally, but districts often have different student information management systems and are unable to effectively use digital records in the transition process. There are also issues of privacy and the ability to transmit large data files, which make electronic transfers cumbersome.

As a result, the new school and classroom teacher must somehow generate new data with assessments or screening tools in order to determine the appropriate instructional level for initial placements and if necessary, interventions at the correct level of difficulty.

The time it takes to perform these diagnostic measures is often dependent on the availability of staff, some of whom may be itinerant and available only at certain times and some that are pulled away from fixed schedules in order to accommodate the need.

The result can be a delay in gathering valuable information that leads to the correct placement of students in both classrooms and in instructional groups with academic intervention supports.

Transcripts for high school and middle school students provide the roadmap for course placements and in the absence of any transcript, it may feel next to impossible to determine the courses needed to keep a student on track for graduation.

There are a multitude of reasons that can account for why there is no transcript available for a student. The student may be coming from another country and is either unable to obtain the transcript, or the information is difficult to translate into our American system for tracking credits.

They may have had sporadic attendance in their previous school, making it difficult for the sending school to send a comprehensive picture of their credits.

There also may be a gap of significant time from when they last attended a school, and the receiving school may have to track down the locations that have the most accurate record of the credits. This may especially be true if the student has been expelled or incarcerated for any length of time.

Finally, a student may be new to the country as an immigrant or refugee and may have very little to no school experience, and certainly no records of any significance available. Districts are faced with the difficult decisions of placing middle and high school students in appropriate programs, knowing that graduation is most likely an impossibility, yet understanding the pressures of raising graduation rates.

SOCIAL EFFECTS OF MOBILITY

Students may experience a variety of social problems resulting from frequent school changes. They range from being completely withdrawn in the new social setting to literally fighting their way to be noticed and accepted. Students may be defiant out of fear that they will change schools again or be apathetic because of past experiences.

Many students display negative attitudes and physical fighting as newcomers in a misguided attempt to assimilate into classrooms that have already gotten underway. Teachers commonly refer to these issues as primary concerns for mobile students as they transition into classrooms.

These types of social effects can also impact students in their adult years, leaving them unable to establish positive, long-term relationships with other adults or peers. Relationships are not viewed as long-term investments, and experience tells them there is less pain involved if they are never formed. There is little experience in knowing and understanding what those healthy connections with adults and peers look like over time.

PARENT VIEWS—DECISIONS AND DILEMMAS

Parents of highly mobile students may make decisions about schools based on highly subjective or false information, or no information at all. Schools may be chosen or avoided simply based on the opinion of others; therefore they may be less likely to enroll their child in specialized programs or magnet schools.

Parents may also circulate their child between schools that are closely located within a geographical area of poverty. This can result in a child moving from one unsuccessful school experience to another on a regular basis. This type of pattern or cycle of movement often becomes very predictable by school level staff members, and over time, can result in perpetuating negative attitudes and perceptions on the part of everyone involved.

Negative interactions with teachers and administrators may contribute to a parent decision to change schools. It may be for a variety of reasons, but the reasons may never be shared with those who can actually resolve the problem.

Clearly the research indicates that student mobility affects the student as well as teachers, administrators, stable student populations, and families. There are community and governmental initiatives that can reduce mobility, but in reality there are few things schools can do to actually reduce mobility to any significant degree.

School administrators and teachers cannot control contributing factors including: rent prices, housing opportunities, divorce rates, mental illness, job loss or availability, and military assignments.

ESSENTIAL IDEAS

- When considering the multiple factors that stem from both poverty and mobility, it is important to focus first on helping people, not the issues that surround them.
- The complexities that arise from the unique situations facing families cannot be categorized into easy groups with blanket solutions.
- Every situation must be treated as unique, seeking first to understand the immediate needs of students and families, followed by the broader mindset of helping all mobile students and families.

FOUR

A Framework for Best Practices

A variety of initiatives have been undertaken in various states and school districts to lessen the negative effects of student mobility. Efforts to reach out to parents and provide information about school attendance and mobility have been realized through community meetings, parent forums, and school liaison contacts.

Other states have coordinated strategies to ensure homeless students have academic, social, and emotional support and can receive help in neighborhood homework centers. Chicago has instituted a mobility awareness campaign designed to inform people about the overall effects of mobility and to encourage stable attendance at one school.

In areas where there are large numbers of migrant workers, initiatives have been put in place to provide family support, literacy development, and tutoring and summer school for migrant students.

Many districts are attempting to keep students in one school if a family moves within a school district in order to minimize student movement, and families are partnered with neighborhood families to encourage positive neighborhood relationships.

FIRST STEPS—TRAINING AND TARGETED STAFF DEVELOPMENT

Schools need to focus their efforts on strategies that reduce the negative effects of student mobility by providing adequate staff development and training for teachers to build awareness of the needs of mobile students and families. Schools can serve as a link for families by establishing partnerships with community agencies and service providers.

Schools are often the first identifiers of family needs and should be ready and able to connect families with appropriate resources to assist them in remaining stable.

A variety of specific strategies can be implemented to welcome new families and students, and schools should have a clear plan of exactly what happens each time a new family comes to register a new student.

When students are entering or exiting a school, records must be transferred quickly and efficiently in order to receive and provide valuable information. Consistent and supportive attendance and discipline policies should be clearly articulated and followed in order to support students as they begin to adjust to a new school environment.

Positive interactions with students and family members are critical when dealing with these issues, and while attendance and discipline must be addressed, great care must be given to build bridges with families and not tear them down before they are ever established.

This also requires administrators to adopt the mentality that schools take responsibility for any child that comes in the door, regardless of the problems they may bring with them. Passing off children with discipline problems to other schools does not work, and the sending school can almost be sure that another incoming child is just as likely to be mobile and present as many of the same or more problems as the one who left.

MAKING CONNECTIONS

There must be consistent outreach programs in order to make initial contacts and maintain positive connections with new families and students. Home visits may be possible, frequent phone calls can be employed, and written communication is always happening between the home and schools in the form of newsletters, notes from teachers, and district information.

PHASES OF ASSIMILATION—BUILDING A LAYERED SYSTEM

As effective practices are put in place, it is necessary to realize there are increasing levels of complexity to consider when designing interventions for welcoming and involving new students and families.

The first phase of interventions is broadly focused and includes general procedures to welcome and facilitate positive adjustments.

The second phase of interventions is more personalized and involves ongoing support and individual contact, such as invitations, phone calls, and more intensive outreach efforts.

The third phase of interventions is required for those who are not adjusting effectively or who remain detached and uninvolved. Students may exhibit negative attitudes or show a strong lack of interest.

This phase requires continued use of personal contacts and extensive outreach, and possibly connections with outside support services such as

Health and Human Services, family counseling, behavioral and mental health professionals, or medical treatment facilities.

STUDENT PLACEMENT—MORE THAN CLASS LISTS

An initial factor to consider is the placement of new students. Students are often placed in classrooms based on maintaining gender or racial balance. Balance may also be limited to equalizing the number of students in a classroom. One teacher at a given grade level may have fewer students in the classroom than the teacher in another classroom at the same grade level, therefore the new student is automatically placed in the room with the lower numbers.

Instead of using these common placement practices, students and families should be asked a variety of questions that elicit information about the child's former school experiences and health history. Students should be assessed with some type of academic screening tools and assigned to classrooms based on achievement levels, including any interventions that support specific areas of need.

PLANNED INSTRUCTION AND PACING

School districts can take steps to ease the academic impact of student mobility by coordinating or pacing the curriculum between schools so students miss minimal instructional content. School districts also need to focus efforts on leaving students in their home school whenever possible despite moves outside of attendance areas.

This can be difficult, especially if districts do not provide transportation. Parents often do not have adequate transportation to take students to a school that may be farther away than one located close to the new residence or attendance area. Some teachers have referred to this type of student as a "boomerang" student. These are students who move between schools or attendance areas on a frequent basis.

DEVELOPMENTAL SUPPORT

Finally, a number of scientific theories support the necessity for effective transition practices for mobile students. In Maslow's model of the hierarchy of needs, survival, self-worth, and a sense of belonging are critical before self-concept and self-actualization can occur, enabling students to then think creatively and utilize higher order thinking skills.

Then there is the transition shock theory in which there are four stages, including loss and disorientation that is brought about by a change in familiar environment. This eventually leads to common symptoms such as resistance to change, discouragement, and withdrawal. With the growing concern of mental health needs for students, this is yet another reason to address the needs of mobile students due to the actual effects on a cognitive level.

This is where the power of teachers and schools is critical to meeting the needs of mobile students. Students must feel they are cared for, welcomed, and accepted. They must feel safe, have adequate nutrition, and experience a sense of belonging to a community. Once these basic needs are met, students can begin to learn and progress academically. School is gradually seen as a haven and a place of safety that then can positively affect student attendance.

Schools must be ready to meet all students where they are, attend to their basic needs, and begin the process of moving them forward academically, socially, and emotionally. When students enter schools at varying times during the school year, it is easy to overlook the need for individualized attention as the transition occurs.

Student mobility is not a new phenomenon, but percentages of mobile students are on the rise in many places and across grade levels.

AREAS OF FOCUS

In an effort to address the needs of mobile student populations, numerous exemplary practices have been identified for schools to assist students as they make transitions into and out of schools. When these practices are collectively identified and broken down by themes, they tend to fall within eight main areas of focus that can serve as the basis for determining the specific areas of needs within a school's current practices. The sections are as follows:

1. Enrollment
2. Academic Placement
3. Student Placement
4. Classroom Connections
5. Family Connections
6. Unique Needs
7. School/Community Connections
8. Exit Transitions

Within the eight identified sections, specific questions have been developed to assess the degree to which current practices are being implemented that follow established best practices.

By completing the questions, strengths can be identified, specific areas of weakness can be addressed, and a Mobility Action Plan can be developed to address the needs of mobile students.

It should be noted that the practices identified within the questions are by no means exhaustive. Schools should always determine which practices are specific to the needs of the school and to both the unique individual and collective needs of students.

It is equally important to determine which practices might currently be in place that are ineffective and need to be eliminated in order to make room for those that better accomplish the goal of helping students make a positive transition.

Many schools could improve a multitude of practices by simply analyzing what does not work and stopping it altogether. Sometimes in the world of education things are made out to be too complex. If it works, continue. If it does not, stop.

QUESTIONS AND ANSWERS

In the next section and throughout the following chapters, a series of questions will be offered to facilitate the process of determining possible needs within the identified areas of focus. When thinking about possible answers to the questions, consider limiting responses to simply Yes or No.

Likert-type responses are appropriate for research that seeks to scale a set of indicators, but the problem with this type of response is that it can give a false sense of positive performance in terms of practical application. For instance, if an answer choice is Almost Always, the results look pretty good if that turns out to be the collective indicator for an entire category.

However, within Almost Always, there are still points where a lack of fidelity may exist. The actual problem may be person specific or system specific, but if the overall indicator is positive, the tendency is to ignore it as a potential area of need and consider it to be "good enough."

The fact of the matter is that practices are either being carried out consistently or they are not. When No becomes the answer, it will allow the drill-down process to occur more effectively, leading to better practices.

ESSENTIAL IDEAS

- This resource seeks to add context around questions that are critical to answer when analyzing the current state of affairs relative to the practices for mobile students.
- As is often the case, questions lead to more questions rather than always arriving at a simple answer. View this as a good outcome if it leads a team toward deeper understanding and implementation.

- By working through a series of questions both planned and un-planned, answers can begin to shape a clearer picture of what is possible, relative to what is.
- Needs assessment instruments can be overwhelming in isolation, but taken in manageable chunks, questions and context can enrich discussions necessary for making lasting changes.

FIVE

The Ins and Outs of Enrollment

The practices contained in this section are often some of the easiest to implement yet are often the least followed on a consistent basis. This is an area that can contain critical gaps in consistency depending on the time of year a student makes a transition.

Effective enrollment practices begin at the front door, and involve everyone from the students to office and maintenance staff. It is not a process that can be left to chance, but rather requires purposeful planning and delegation.

Families must find a welcoming environment and be assisted by key people in the office such as a secretary or office aide whose primary responsibility is to welcome new families and assist them with registration procedures. It may also require a lot of time, and bilingual assistance should be provided on site whenever necessary.

The people who are the critical players in the initial contact must have the ability to make everyone feel as if they are the most important people to walk in the door that day, using time and patience to meet the needs of individual families.

FACILITY CONSIDERATIONS—WHERE DO WE GO?

The physical structure of a building should always be considered when looking through the lens of a newcomer. If security measures have been developed that have altered the entrance or procedures for a school, there must be elements in place to foster a welcoming environment, while still supporting the goals of appropriate security.

The layout of many schools serves as an automatic barrier if the initial design was poorly laid out, or if renovations were done without this consideration. Think about the entrance of your school with these questions in mind:

- Is there a sign posted next to a buzzer or external speaker that says, "Welcome to our school, we are glad you're here. Please ring for service." Or does it say, "All visitors must report to office. No exceptions!"

Consider the location of parking lots in proximity to school offices. There are often multiple entrances for larger schools, which may provide a set of confusing options when determining which door leads to the main entrance.

- Is visitor parking readily available and identified for people visiting the school?
- If the office is not located near the main entrance of the school, are there clear directions that visibly guide people to the right location?

SCHOOL CLIMATE—FIRST IMPRESSIONS MATTER

Public speakers know there is a very small window of time to capture and keep the attention of an audience. The same is true of school visitors. When people arrive and enter a school, the climate of the overall building is evident within minutes, and a first impression can leave a lasting impression that colors every interaction that follows.

Consider these key questions as you think about the overall feeling of your school:

- Are classroom teachers and support staff as eager to meet students in the middle of the year as they were during the scheduled Open House at the beginning of the year?
- Do the right faces belong to the first faces?

One of the biggest problem areas associated with first impressions is the overall culture of the school office. Some of the most efficient people in the office are not necessarily the ones to offer the warmest welcomes. It may be due to the level of activity going on at any given time, the ability to multitask and respond to a new or stressful situation, or simply having a low tolerance level for those who are considered to be late arrivals.

Schools need to know where the responsibility lies for greeting anyone who comes into the school and make sure the people assigned to the role are appropriately trained so there is consistency of service every time.

Secretaries and administrative assistants are often assigned to this role because of their proximity, but that does not mean it has to automatically fall within their duties. For some, this may be a natural strength, but for others, the best fit may be a simple greeting with a smile while they call for the person who can provide a truly warm and welcoming experience. Either way, it should not be a random event or left up to chance.

- Are there specific staff members in your school who are designated to assist new families when they arrive at the school office?
- Can all staff members clearly articulate their role in the enrollment process?

ENROLLMENT PRACTICES AND PROCEDURES

After students and families walk through the door, the next steps usually involve some type of paperwork necessary to enroll students in school. Parents are required to provide proof of identification, immunization, and other information relevant to enrollment.

This is often a highly stressful part of the process for families for a number of different reasons, most of which can be anticipated and alleviated if adequate preparation has occurred.

DOCUMENTS AND DOLLARS

One of the first areas of stress occurs when parents are asked to produce documents that they may no longer have due to multiple moves, or due to the nature of the move. If the family has moved as a result of domestic violence, eviction, or other trauma, the move may have occurred quite suddenly, and personal items may have been left behind.

At the point the school office requests the documents, the adult enrolling the child may not want to disclose the actual reason for not having the documents, and immediately feels the stress of appearing unprepared.

The rules of the game may have also changed from place to place if the family has undergone frequent moves between states, where there may be a difference in what is required at the time of enrollment.

Stress can also be heightened if the process requires people to sit and wait for long periods of time, particularly if there are young children in the group. Schools often have packets of forms ready at the beginning of the year for Kindergarten Round-up, Open House, Walkthrough Night, or specific enrollment events, but as the year progresses, supplies may not have been replenished or packaged together in anticipation of more students.

If the wait time is prolonged, families may begin to feel like they are causing an inconvenience, particularly if the young children become loud and chaos ensues.

- After the initial start of the year, are the enrollment forms still easily accessible?

- Is there a comfortable place to complete forms and ask questions?
- Is all relevant information for new students and families easily accessible through the school website?
- Are families given a complete list of supplies students need to begin school?
- If supplies are unavailable or unobtainable, does the school provide them?

A second major area of stress occurs when parents are asked to pay for unexpected items during the enrollment process. Fee structures vary widely from school to school and district to district.

In addition to paying for school lunches, which is usually an expected school cost, parents also may be asked to pay for unexpected items such as P.E. uniforms, activity cards, and instrument rentals.

It is incumbent upon school districts to make sure established federal and state laws and district guidelines are followed when dealing with any student fees. It is also important to provide clear information and access to any fee waiver documents that may be applicable to a family's socioeconomic qualifications, allowing them to have fees waived or reduced.

- Are parents asked to pay additional fees when enrolling in school that might be unexpected?
- Is information regarding fee waivers available at the time of enrollment?

LANGUAGE AND CULTURE

The next point of stress can occur when there is a language barrier that prevents a family from communicating effectively with the school office. If there is no interpreter on site, or a translation service is unavailable, the process may be delayed and parents may feel like they are creating an inconvenience for the school or they may be offended by the lack of accommodations.

The language itself can also present a barrier if it is one that has not typically been encountered by the school, and if staff members are not familiar with the culture or language before that point. It may be necessary to quickly look up common characteristics of the culture, such as expectations for greetings, cultural norms with who commonly speaks for the family, and any cultural customs that should be considered.

- Are translated materials or the services of a translator available as needed?
- If a translator is not available on site, are there clear procedures for contacting one?

- Are staff members culturally proficient when a variety of cultures are represented in the community?

If a language barrier exists, there may also be a high level of anxiety depending on the community and a family's perception of how welcomed they may be. Immigration fears, extreme culture shifts, and racial prejudice should always be considered when helping families from different cultures enroll children in school in order to assure a positive experience.

ILLITERACY—AN OVERLOOKED REALITY

Most often, staff members who deal with the enrollment of a child assume the adult is literate and fully capable of completing written forms and paperwork. However, this may not always be the case, and staff members should be aware that assistance might be welcomed, as adults need to both read and understand what they are asked to complete.

Forms and information should be checked for readability levels, and ideally should not be above an eighth grade level of comprehension.

- Do families receive written and verbal information about school procedures?
- Are materials simple and easy to read with an average readability at or below eighth grade?
- Are families given clear information about how to contact the school office?

FAMILY STRUCTURES

Another layer of consideration should be included within the enrollment process as schools deal with a wide variety of family structures. Students come from many different family structures, and staff members need to be aware of and sensitive to those differences when addressing students and the greater topic of families.

Some students may live with only one parent. Others may live with grandparents, great grandparents, or a legal guardian. Some students may have parents of the same sex, and others may be living completely on their own.

Regardless of the scenario, schools need to remember that students come from diverse backgrounds, some of which are different than our own. Our lenses have to be wide enough to take those factors into account as we establish practices to meet the needs of all families when they come to enroll a child in school.

- Do enrollment forms and communication tools reflect options or information that encompasses diverse family structures?

CONSISTENCY

Another factor to consider as practices and procedures are reviewed is the consistency with which they are performed. If procedures have been established, it is much easier to be consistent with every family and every child as they enroll in school. If they have not, it is easy to leave out some steps that are critical to making a successful transition.

- Are consistent procedures followed for enrolling all new students?
- Are school tours provided for all new students and families?
- Are systems in place for notifying existing staff members and students when new students arrive?
- Is the classroom or homeroom teacher personally introduced to the new student and family?

ESSENTIAL IDEAS

- As students make the transition into a new school it is important to maintain a consistent set of procedures in order to provide the best experience possible for every family, every time.
- Staff members must be committed to providing a welcoming environment as soon as people get out of the car to come into the school, and must do so no matter what time of year the transition takes place.
- Every child and every family deserves to feel like they are an important part of the new school environment regardless of how long they may attend.
- The first experience can make all the difference for every experience that comes after the point of enrollment.
- If families experience high levels of stress and anxiety during their initial visits to the school, the odds are not good for establishing any kind of lasting relationship.
- Staff members must be aware of diverse cultural and family structures that may be very different from their own, and understand how their perceptions may influence the transition process.

SIX

The Ins and Outs of Academic Placement and Student Learning

When students are welcomed into a new school and classroom, specific time and attention must be given to initial placement decisions. Decisions cannot be based solely on keeping classroom sizes even, racial groups evenly distributed, or the lottery of which teacher's number is up for receiving a new student.

Schools must have academic placement practices in place in order to make the best determination based on data, rather than subjective factors that may not result in positive academic transitions.

School-level practices must also be supported by district-level practices such as instructional coherence and the existence of a viable and guaranteed curriculum. Many districts provide clear guidelines for teachers on instructional pacing, which reflect a variety of timelines including semester, quarterly, monthly, or even weekly guidelines. However, knowing clearly what students are to know and demonstrate is most important in assuring the ability to effectively plan for instruction.

This type of curriculum framework can reduce the negative effects of intradistrict mobility to some degree, particularly if teachers are part of the development of instructional guidelines and common assessments.

However, a practice that may be even more effective is to provide students and families with the framework of concepts that will be covered in the course of an entire school year. This provides an expanded picture of the true breadth and depth of learning that will take place, and may reinforce the importance of stability related to academic success.

OBTAINING AND SENDING STUDENT ACADEMIC RECORDS

Schools should make every effort to process requests for student records as quickly as possible. However, this is often a practice that can be significantly delayed due to a variety of reasons. Some transfers of records may be delayed due to the sheer volume of data being transferred due to high mobility.

Other delays may stem from inadequate personnel to perform these types of tasks. Hopefully the days of delaying record transfers due to unpaid fines or unreturned books and materials are over, even though schools often feel there is very little leverage to help this related problem.

- Are requests for student records or new files processed in a short amount of time?
- Have adequate processes been put in place to assure records are not delayed in the sending or receiving of information?
- Do office staff members understand the importance of student file information in reviewing academic, social, and attendance data for new students?
- Does the information sent from your school contain information that makes subsequent placements easier for receiving schools (checklists, benchmark data, progress notes)?

ASSESSING FOR PLACEMENT

If academic or attendance data are delayed for students when requesting and receiving records from other districts, schools must be able to adapt quickly to effectively assess an accurate achievement level in core subjects and place students in the classroom setting that will meet their needs most accurately.

A variety of options exist within the use of available summative and formative assessments, either through a traditional paper/pencil format in the classroom or through web-based products that are widely used specifically for placement purposes.

- Are there designated assessments used for the specific purpose of placing students based on academic needs?
- Are specific assessments given to determine a student's current reading level?
- Are specific assessments given to determine a student's current math level?
- Can specialists such as reading teachers or ELL (English Language Learner) teachers take the data and quickly design a plan that is targeted directly at the most critical areas of learning?

- Are the needs of the student specifically matched to the instructional strengths of the classroom teacher?

TEACHER RESISTANCE

When a new student arrives, significant time is required to assess and plan for student needs. They may or may not fit neatly within established instructional groups for intervention, remediation, or acceleration.

Teachers may question the relevance of devoting time for placement activities, particularly if a student has already experienced a high degree of mobility. By the time they are assessed, placed, and instructed for any length of time, they may be gone. So why try?

The reason is simple. For a student who has or will continue to experience mobility, every day counts. Every opportunity for learning at the correct level of difficulty is crucial for any type of cumulative success they have throughout the course of the educational journey.

Due to the number of days and months when students may miss instruction, the number of days and months they do not miss become exponentially more important.

ESSENTIAL IDEAS

- Students must be placed in classrooms based on academic need, not by chance or convenience.
- There may be significant gaps in achievement due to mobility and every opportunity to gain lost ground can mean the difference between failure and success for a child.
- Students may be well ahead of where a new classroom is and require significant differentiation of instruction and content to keep them moving ahead.
- Placing students in a classroom that expects them to sit and wait to catch up or move ahead is unacceptable and can be avoided if steps are taken to assess current levels of proficiency.

SEVEN

The Ins and Outs of Student Placement Decisions

In addition to academic placement factors, other decisions must be made as well, taking into consideration a number of classroom realities. The other aspect of student placement decisions lies in the "how" of the decision-making process.

Schools must determine whether placement decisions will rest solely with the principal or head administrator, or if they will be made collaboratively with the help of a team of people.

COLLABORATIVE DECISIONS

Collaboration for enrollment placements focuses on the importance of making decisions with careful thought rather than doing what is simple and obvious. This requires a high level of commitment on the part of the entire staff.

Teachers have to be willing to work in a classroom that may have more students than another classroom at the same grade level.

Specialists have to be willing to accommodate schedules that change and flex with the addition of a new student in a classroom that does not have all of the group members conveniently located in one room.

Secretaries have to be willing to wait for team decisions to be made rather than hurrying through the process in order to update lists, input data in the student management system, and get papers off of the desk and into the file drawer.

Placement decisions can no longer be made based on making things fair and even. The old adage, "What is fair is not always equal, and what is equal is not always fair," must be a reality of the collaborative decision-making process.

COMMON PLACEMENT FACTORS—GENDER BALANCE

One of the most common factors that influences placement decisions is the gender balance of student lists. In other words, how many boys and how many girls are in classrooms where multiple classrooms exist at every grade level? This may be a holdover practice that has stayed in place as part of how things have always been done, rather than reflecting on the purpose for doing so.

While it is good practice to have a reasonable gender balance, it may not be as important as it is sometimes made out to be, particularly if academic needs outweigh the need for balance.

Unfortunately, this type of factor can also take on a higher level of importance due to the perceived need to maintain a sense of fairness and equity for teachers and their classroom populations.

That is why it is essential to consider collaborative decisions in order to determine correct placements for new students. In making decisions this way, it is no longer the secretary making a placement decision based on numbers, but rather a team of people making the decision based on student need.

- Are placement decisions based heavily on gender balance?
- Does a team of people have input on placement decisions or is it isolated to one person?

COMMON PLACEMENT FACTORS—RACIAL BALANCE

Another common factor that influences enrollment placement is racial balance. This is quite similar to maintaining gender balance, and seeks to make things fair and equitable between classrooms.

With the best of intentions, it may be due to multiple ethnicities represented at a school and the need to maintain balance for the sake of diversity.

It may also be due to the need for efficient grouping of students for language classes or remedial intervention services and scheduling. If teachers who serve in these areas are only available during limited times throughout the school day, it may be necessary to group students accordingly to provide adequate services.

Scheduling needs provide an opportunity to review nontraditional or more creative options for scheduling support staff such as staggering their starting and ending times to provide for blocks of uninterrupted classroom instruction. School districts are finding success in this option, providing greater flexibility for meeting the learning needs of students.

While scheduling is certainly a reality and a consideration, it should not be the only determining factor for placing a student in a given classroom.

- Are placement decisions based heavily on racial balance?
- Does racial balance equate with scheduling of services?
- Is there a lack of racial balance because of scheduling and services?
- Have other creative measures been considered to provide viable alternatives for services?

COMMON PLACEMENT FACTORS—INDIVIDUALIZED EDUCATIONAL PROGRAM (IEP)

Students receiving special education services require a dual lens for placement with needs that connect to both the general education classroom and the special education classroom. Teachers with expertise and experience in a particular area within the scope of special education services should always be the first consideration, however a child may also have unique emotional or social needs that factor into the placement decision.

If current IEP documents are not readily available, it is important to get as much information as possible from the parent, or a school can request permission to make contact with the former school for some basic information.

Some parents are able to provide a wealth of information if they have been active participants in their child's educational program. Others may not be able to provide as much detailed information, having only been aware of the basics of their child's program such as scheduling and room assignment.

In isolated cases, parents may choose not to indicate that a child has been receiving special education services. They may see the change in schools as an opportunity for a "fresh start" and perceive that the services that had been in place are no longer necessary.

They may have had negative experiences with the former school and want to eliminate that factor from a new placement, or they may believe the new school may not see the academic needs a child has demonstrated in the past.

The opposite scenario can also occur when a parent indicates a child has been receiving services in an effort to obtain additional help for a child, particularly if a child has been denied services in the past that a parent believes are warranted.

Both scenarios can lead to an awkward position for the school when official records are obtained and either situation has to be adjusted.

- Have questions been developed as part of the enrollment process, specific to supplemental or primary services such as special education, English Language Learner (ELL), gifted, or intervention services if educational records are unavailable?

THE TEAM

There are a variety of people in a school who can be considered to be part of an enrollment team, and the needs of a school will somewhat dictate who the appropriate personnel should be. The makeup of the team can also change as situations arise that call for different areas of expertise.

Some likely team members may be administrators, classroom teachers, counselors, social workers, cultural liaisons, special education teachers, ELL teachers, and specialists.

This model of collaboration requires a commitment of time on the part of team members and the flexibility to meet when the need arises. The team may change over time to distribute responsibility and leadership across a school, but the central purpose of collaborative decision making for enrollment must remain as a central focus and core purpose.

- Are people willing to serve on a school enrollment team?
- Are the unique characteristics and expertise needed for the enrollment team identified for your school?

ESSENTIAL IDEAS

- Collaborative perspectives on enrollment can help schools make good placement decisions for students.
- A collaborative decision-making structure requires additional time and energy, so teams need to be kept at a manageable number of people for practical reasons such as scheduling and coordination of meeting times.
- The benefits of this decision-making model can impact the entire school when there is a shared vision of how students are placed.
- The result of this structure will be a much stronger emphasis on "our students" versus "my students" when looking at the classroom placement picture as a whole.

EIGHT

The Ins and Outs of
Classroom Connections

Classroom connections require critical steps in helping students form immediate connections with peers and adults in the new school. This is another area that is typically well done at the beginning of the year, but as the year progresses the same level of attention is not given to this important step and students are at risk of feeling disconnected and disoriented.

The other essential component in this area is providing the training necessary for teachers and students to carry out the practices well, and understanding how vitally important the practices are for helping every new student.

STUDENT CONNECTIONS

Being a buddy to a new student may be seen as a privilege or something fun to do as a classroom helper. But students need to understand the importance of their role in helping a new student connect to the classroom. If students understand the rationale behind their critical function, they can perform their duty with a newfound sense of importance.

It is also important for them to realize this when the new student to whom they have been assigned is less than popular or difficult to befriend. If the only goal is to provide a new friend, the student buddies may quickly abandon their posts. But if they see the bigger picture, they will understand and be able to maintain some objectivity and sense of service in helping a new person.

- Are all students assigned a peer buddy that has been trained for this role?

- Are non-English speaking students assigned a peer buddy who speaks their home language?
- Are a variety of students trained to be buddies in order to match new students based on common interests and personalities?

TEACHER CONNECTIONS

One of the elements that can often be absent from preparing for mobile students is adequate training for teachers and clearly defined procedures that are an expectation for everyone in terms of helping a child become oriented to a new school and classroom.

Teachers are often expected to have effective practices in place as part of their classroom procedures for new students, yet have done so with very little training and guidance.

This leads to random practices that are not aligned for entire schools, and leaves the successful transition of mobile students up to the relative expertise of the teacher. In other words, the procedures are only as good as the teacher causes them to be.

There may be wide variability from classroom to classroom based on experience, expertise, and awareness. There may even be situations where some teachers are simply more skilled at receiving new students and may enjoy the challenges presented with each new arrival.

Rather than expecting all teachers to be experts at helping mobile students, the option of having resident experts could be considered as an alternative when planning for student placement practices.

- Are there consistent practices in place that guide the student orientation process in every classroom?
- Are classroom teachers trained in specific strategies focused on receiving new students in their class and in the school?

There can be a disconnect between helping students make good connections within their classroom and how students are connected with other staff members in the school. Students interact with many teachers and staff members outside of the classroom but may not be formally introduced or oriented to the other classrooms where they will be during the course of the school day.

Specialists often feel disconnected from the transition process for receiving new students and can be surprised when a teacher arrives at their door with an additional student in the mix. They may be unprepared with materials, seating, or other items that a student needs to fully participate. The same can be true of accommodations that need to be made for special education students or English Language Learners.

- Are students introduced to other teachers they may have during the course of their day?

- Do students have an opportunity to share personal information with all teachers who are part of their daily schedule?

EVERYONE MATTERS

Specialists and support staff are critical members of the team when it comes to making all new students and families feel welcomed. When the full course of the day is considered, a student makes many stops where they encounter a variety of adults. They meet staff members in the morning as they get ready to enter a school. Then they encounter other adults in the hallways during transitions and during lunch and recess. Finally, they may see others during special classes and after school.

One factor that seems to be very effective for mobile students is to have another teacher or staff member other than their classroom teacher serve as a connecting point during the course of the day. Through this practice students are connected to both their primary teacher as well as another significant adult in the school. It provides an additional opportunity to form positive relationships with the adults in the building.

- Are students assigned to an adult mentor other than the classroom teacher?

Many schools have formal volunteer mentoring programs available for students, so connections with other adults may occur because of those specific programs. But if there are no formal mentoring programs in place, assigning someone specific is a great way to connect students and adults more quickly.

Planning for connections with multiple adults allows for greater collective responsibility for new students across the entire staff. Custodians, paraprofessionals, librarians, school nurses, and others can play a specific part in the process of affecting the entire climate of a school through the shared goal of connecting with all students.

SIMPLE DOTS—ONE IDEA WITH BIG IMPACT

Some schools have adopted the practice of listing all of the students in the school on a wall chart. The adults in the school are asked to simply place a dot next to any students they know by name, and can identify one thing they know specific to that child.

The goal is to make sure that every student has a dot next to a name and can be personally recognized by name by more people in the school than just their homeroom teacher or schedule teachers.

SAFETY AND SECURITY PROCEDURES

As students enter a new school, safety and security must be a high priority both in terms of the individual student as well as the entire school. Many procedures are learned and practiced at the beginning of the year, but as time goes by they are not reinforced regularly, or not reviewed at the point when a new student enters.

A fire drill is a perfect example of a procedure that is often overlooked and one that new students are not privy to until the time the drill is held. Imagine if a drill was held on the very first morning of the first day at a new school. This might create a very alarming feeling for many students.

- Are all students given a tour of the school when they arrive no matter when they arrive during the day or during the school year?
- Do all students have a school orientation to learn procedures for areas outside of their classroom, such as the lunchroom, playground, or media center?
- Do students know emergency procedures such as evacuation drills?
- Do students know expectations for secured entrances and exits such as not opening doors for adults who are waiting to enter?
- Do parents of new students know school procedures and expectations for safety and security measures?

ESSENTIAL IDEAS

- Students must be given multiple opportunities to connect over a period of time, not just on the first day of arrival.
- In order to make effective connections quickly, it is important for all adults to see themselves as a vital part of the process.
- Students need to know the adults in their school and understand the procedures and expectations for all areas of the school as part of their school day.
- Regardless of when students are enrolled, they need to feel safe, secure, and connected.
- When these practices happen quickly and effectively, students are much more likely to feel secure at their new school and are better prepared to begin learning.

NINE

The Ins and Outs of Family Connections

When new families arrive on the school doorstep, they are met with a myriad of reactions. Many of those reactions are dependent upon things completely unrelated to specific action steps and beliefs about how every family should be received when they come into the school.

Their reception may hinge on how they are dressed, what language they speak, or how young children are behaving in the office. It may depend on the perceived educational or socioeconomic level of the parent or how quickly they fill out the required forms and provide the necessary information for enrollment.

But the true question for schools is in asking if the goal is to genuinely connect with families, or to just present the illusion of wanting to connect with families.

There is a big difference between the two camps. Wanting to connect with families requires action, extra time, inconvenience, and extended hours beyond the school day.

The appearance of wanting to connect with families lies in brochures, newsletters, and one-way communication. Those tools are not bad, but if used alone without further personal follow up, they certainly are not going to get the job done of bringing families through the door in meaningful ways.

DESIGNATED ROLES

As suggested earlier, one of the most critical steps in providing consistent experiences for families when enrolling children in school is having staff members assigned specifically to that role. Rarely will one person be enough to assume this role given the complexities of daily schedules.

The school day should be reviewed to determine which people would be available during blocks of time, meaning they could be interrupted or their duties could be easily shifted to another person with little notice.

- Have staff members been designated to serve as point people for new families when they come to the school to enroll?
- Have schedules been reviewed to provide the best coverage possible for welcoming families at any point in the school day?

This requires a willingness on the part of staff members to deal with occasional short-term inconveniences in order to accomplish the long-term goals of the school. It also requires a spirit of service to students and families without regard to the expected duration of a student's enrollment. Great care should be taken to choose people who demonstrate this level of service.

DUAL ORIENTATION

When families have completed the actual enrollment process, it is important to provide a quality orientation that captures both sides of the school experience. Information should be provided that covers both what students will learn and how they will learn it as well as information about the place where they will learn it.

- Are families given an orientation that covers both academic and nonacademic information?
- Are parents aware of the learning expectations for the grade level of their child?
- Are parents informed about the educational intervention and extension opportunities available for their child?

Much of this information is widely available on school and district websites. But as an assurance, important information should be reviewed purposefully so parents and families are aware of essential expectations. Information about safety, security, and bullying should also be highlighted as a proactive, preventative measure.

With the recent events in the greater school picture, these are some of the areas families question first, particularly if there have been issues related to domestic violence or custody issues.

TECHNOLOGY AND INFORMATION

Effective transition practices for mobile students take time, but technology can be a great tool in developing informational items that can be shown to families during their visit and can be made available via school and district websites.

This also allows greater flexibility if staff do not have to be physically present to provide information, and greater consistency when the message stays the same with every presentation.

- Is technology being leveraged as a tool to provide information and opportunities for parents and families?
- Is the information provided through school and district websites up-to-date and accurate?

SCHOOL AND COMMUNITY CONNECTIONS

After the initial transition takes place, the next step is to connect parents and families with the greater school community and other parents and families. Many schools have parents in volunteer roles with the primary focus of welcoming newcomers. In some instances, the local parent organization coordinates this kind of effort.

As part of the enrollment process, parents can indicate their willingness to be contacted by another parent to receive additional information, and to serve as a resource if there are additional questions. This allows parents to ask questions of other parents if they may otherwise hesitate to ask the school.

- Is a parent from the school who is identified as a family liaison available to contact new families?
- Are new families specifically invited to attend school events?
- Are families encouraged to volunteer at school by being provided with a written list of volunteer opportunities?

CONTINUING CONNECTIONS

Once children have been enrolled and the initial process is complete, a period of adjustment follows. Students begin to come home with homework, informational items, and possibly problems. In order to assess how the transition is progressing, schools can provide a follow-up phone call or purposeful contact with new families.

This allows parents to ask additional questions and provide input on how things are going for their child and for them. It also may provide additional information relevant to the family that can be helpful to the school.

- Does the school administrator or other staff member contact new families to help with the continued transition?

Parents who are making transitions with jobs, living arrangements, and family structures may welcome the chance to let the school know how things are going, knowing the transitions may also be affecting their child at school. This may also provide the opportunity to connect with staff members whose primary responsibility is to support the social and emotional needs of children and families, such as counselors and social workers.

Parents may hesitate to contact the school for continued support, but when the opportunity is offered to them proactively, it can make all the difference.

ESSENTIAL IDEAS

- As families and students enter a new school, it is not enough to ensure that forms are completed and tours are given.
- Connections must go deeper and last longer in order to establish a continued positive experience at school.
- Students must be connected to classrooms, and families must be connected with schools.
- Connections must run between school and parent, and from parent to parent.
- When families feel like they are part of the school community in the wider sense, it may reduce the likelihood of further movement.
- While there is no guarantee, the overall perception of what it means to be part of a school community may become more positive in the process.

TEN

The Ins and Outs of Unique Needs

When new students come to school, many of their needs are quite apparent. However, some of the details may be left out of the picture if records are not readily available from the sending school. Parents may omit information, thinking their child deserves a new start, believing somehow the areas they have struggled in over time will magically disappear in a new school.

Parents may not have the wherewithal to communicate information regarding health concerns, learning accommodations, and language needs. Special education needs may go unmentioned because of prior negative experiences or the assumption that the necessary details are transferred automatically from school to school in a timely manner.

There is also the mindset that the bare minimum is enough when enrolling a child. The parent may feel it is up to the new school to find out the details, and therefore it is not seen as part of parental responsibility.

DELAYED INFORMATION

Unfortunately, delaying information that assists in making appropriate initial placements is not only detrimental to helping the students have a successful transition, but it serves to delay academic progress even further, contributing to a picture that may already be quite dismal.

Any delay equates to lost time in helping students gain ground they may still be able to recover. It may be difficult for schools to feel a sense of urgency in gathering this type of information when it does not come quickly from either another school or the parent. It may be easier to plead ignorance later if the information never comes and the child remains in the school. If they do not stay, it may not be viewed as a lost cause because it already was perceived as such even before the child started.

THE RIGHT QUESTIONS FROM THE RIGHT PEOPLE

In order to get the right information, the right questions must be asked during the enrollment process. If a language barrier exists, the right questions have to be posed in the right language to get the information necessary for placing students in appropriate programs.

If health concerns are evident, the school nurse has to become involved immediately, and special education teachers need to plug students into schedules shortly after initial placement, not after weeks have passed, even if it is within legal time limits.

ADDITIONAL CONSIDERATIONS—HEALTH NEEDS

Forms are an efficient way to get information from incoming new families. However, if a parent checks "yes" in a box that asks if a child has medical needs that should be noted, a process must be in place to assure that the healthcare staff member is available to follow up for more details.

The range of information varies widely from student to student in terms of medication needs, complex care requirements for tracheotomy tubes or feeding tubes, food allergies, and a whole host of other conditions that require medical attention at school.

The next part of the process has to provide connections between the information that is noted by the healthcare staff and all of the relevant staff members in the rest of the school who should be aware of the need.

For instance, if a child has asthma and requires an inhaler, it is critical that the physical education teacher is aware and can follow the asthma action plan protocol for that child. If a student is prone to seizures, custodians, food service staff, and paraprofessionals must know the information so they can respond in hallways, cafeterias, and on the playground if necessary.

- Are student health needs communicated to the school health office and classroom teacher upon enrollment?
- Are other staff members notified about health needs relevant to their assignments?
- Do parents know how to reach the school office and health professionals, and do they know the plan that is in place for their child's needs while they are at school?

Parents need to feel confident that their children are going to receive appropriate care for health-related issues. Some needs may be minor while others are quite significant and require careful monitoring over time.

There is a fine line when dealing with student health needs in terms of privacy and sharing information with appropriate staff members. Care should be taken to involve those who need to know, while still protecting the privacy of the child. Parents are partners in the process, and should be aware of all staff members and students who will know information and the expectations for responding to the child's needs.

LANGUAGE

As discussed earlier, as students and families come to school to enroll, there may be a variety of complexities due to language needs. The need for translated forms and information cannot be overstated. However, if the language needs continue to be part of the student's regular school day, it is important for arrangements to be made to accommodate those needs as efficiently as possible.

- Does the school have an interpreter on staff that can accommodate the needs of the students during the school day?
- If an interpreter is not readily available, can other accommodations be made to meet the needs of the child until one can be obtained?

Language needs may differ if they stem from special education accommodations such as a visual or hearing impairment. Students may require Braille translations or ongoing Braille instruction for a visual impairment. Students with a hearing loss may need the services of sign language interpretation and instruction.

While these services are somewhat different in scope than students who speak a language other than English, the bottom line is the need for students to be able to effectively communicate throughout their school day and during related activities as appropriate.

In larger, metropolitan areas, these services may be easy to find, but in more rural or isolated areas it may be very difficult to find any of the above types of interpreter and translation services. Technology can be an invaluable tool in providing translation services, and can assist with interpreter needs if distance-learning capabilities exist.

There are more and more online services that can be utilized to fill this need, and it may be necessary for a school district to invest in training if a long-term need exists.

MAKING ACCOMMODATIONS

Learning accommodations may be necessary due to both IEP goals or because of nonspecial education learning needs. However, information regarding both of these aspects is often difficult to get in an efficient and timely manner for a variety of reasons.

One of the best ways to meet the needs of a new student quickly is to ask the sending school to fax a copy of the current IEP if one has not yet been sent, or if it can be expedited apart from the regular request for records. Parents may be able to provide some information, but it is often limited or not specific to actual instructional strategies. As discussed earlier, this is a critical part of the learning environment for the student.

Once this information is gathered, it is equally important to share this information with other staff members who may also need to be aware of specific accommodations.

For instance if a struggling reader is asked to read aloud as part of music class, the music teacher may needlessly embarrass a child just at the point when they are trying to include them as a new student. An art teacher may not be aware of a language barrier and may ask a child to follow specific directions as part of an art project, yet the student is not able to comprehend the directions or the sequence of completion.

These and many other examples point out the need for effective communication between larger groups of staff members than what is often considered when new students enroll in school.

- Is basic information shared with all relevant staff members in order to facilitate appropriate accommodations in multiple classrooms for new students?

NONACADEMIC ACCOMMODATIONS

Other related accommodations which are not directly related to academics may be just as critical. Students may need mental health services, behavioral accommodations such as behavior plans and appropriate calming spaces, and occupational or physical therapy.

Students may have needs related to physical accessibility if they have assistive devices such as wheelchairs, crutches, or walkers. They may have hearing aids, require amplification equipment, or may need toileting assistance.

Depending on the services already in place, it may be no problem for a school to adjust to providing the necessary physical accommodations for a new student. However, if the needs are new to a school, there may need to be some significant steps taken to both obtain staff members and train them to perform the necessary duties as part of the accommodations.

- Is there a process in place for noting and providing for specific physical accommodations which may be necessary for new students?

SOCIAL AND EMOTIONAL ACCOMMODATIONS

Students need to be able to learn in spaces that are conducive to their academic and physical needs. Students also may have social and emotional needs which impact their school day, and schools may or may not be aware of these unique needs at the point of enrollment. Many students enroll and re-enroll in the same schools over time, and as they do, schools are well aware of their behavioral and social needs.

If a student has significant behavioral and social needs, parents may not readily share information for fear of their child being "labeled" as a troublemaker or as different from the other children. Students may be dealing with gender identification issues, mental health needs, or ongoing issues stemming from abuse or trauma.

If students are physically or verbally aggressive, the needs may become apparent very quickly, allowing a school to ask additional questions or request additional information from prior schools. They also may simply be required to act quickly based on the immediacy and severity of the needs.

Students may need a recovery room if they have frequent outbursts and may require a comprehensive behavioral plan that includes multiple teachers and classrooms. They may also have specific "triggers" that should be avoided if they are antecedents to outbursts or incidents of extreme aggression.

- Are processes in place for making accommodations quickly and efficiently such as activating Student Assistance Teams or Response to Intervention protocols?

Students may be entering school after being incarcerated or spending time in some type of juvenile detention facility. They may have probation terms and may even be under some type of house arrest with an electronic monitoring device, such as an ankle bracelet, that indicates their status to the rest of the world.

This may be quite common in some schools, while in others it presents a brand new challenge in terms of helping a student assimilate into the general population. Teachers may be uncomfortable with the situation and need to know exactly how to handle the unique needs of students who enter school in this type of situation.

ESSENTIAL IDEAS

- When new students enroll, services required for individual accommodations may already be in place if other students require similar services.

- The needs of some students may present new challenges for schools academically, physically, socially, and emotionally.
- Some of the needs displayed by a child may be "old hat" for the new school, but some may be brand new and staff members may be caught unprepared to adjust to those needs.
- Schools must be able to respond with flexibility and agility to meet the needs of all students, taking the steps necessary to adapt learning spaces and build staff expertise.
- Schools must establish a collective expectation to do whatever it takes, regardless of when a child enrolls and how long attendance is maintained at a school.

ELEVEN

The Ins and Outs of Community Connections

Families in transition require extra support when helping them connect to a new school and a new community. They are often in need of resources and are not familiar with the channels needed to access those resources. This type of situation affects the level of readiness a student has for starting school successfully in a new place.

For instance, if the family left the former school abruptly, students may not have school supplies or even a backpack for their things. If they were living with another family member and had to leave quickly because of an adversarial situation, they may not have taken the few belongings they had or may have left with the intention of being able to return after a "cooling off" period.

Students may or may not have their clothing or things such as hats and mittens during the winter months. Furniture may be a luxury item, resulting in children sleeping on the floor, or if there is a bed, multiple siblings may occupy that space, resulting in poor sleep and bedtime routines. Families may be living in shelters or temporary locations with little access to items for meeting the most basic needs.

Those types of details are often not disclosed to school personnel for fear of authorities being called or for fear that they will be judged to be poor parents if basic needs are not being met.

But what teachers may see are the students who are falling asleep during class, those who are having difficulty paying attention to instruction, and the disheveled appearance they have as they enter the classroom in the morning, most likely more than a few minutes late. They may also be hungry, have some degree of body odor, and may make frequent trips to the nurse's office.

Teachers and staff members may not make connections between what is seen in the classroom and the other factors outside of school which influence the ability of a child to perform at their best in school.

BASIC NEEDS

If the true goal is to support mobile students in transition, families need to have opportunities to access local resources and the people who can help them connect quickly in the new setting.

Families need to know how to get information about the school and community for childcare, after school clubs, and opportunities to interact with the school. They may still be in need of housing at the time of arrival and may need basic items of food and clothing while the transition process is completed.

School districts need to make sure specific contact people are designated for the purpose of coordination of services and resources within buildings as well as between buildings in larger districts. In doing so, schools are better able to assist families, and in turn, support mobile students as they begin to make local connections.

If families are moving within a community, they may already be aware of resources and services that exist, but if they are brand new they may be unaware of the resources or may not know how to access them. This need underscores the importance of healthy school and community partnerships that support students and families, and the need to coordinate efforts to provide assistance at the time of need.

- Are materials about community resources and contacts made available to new families at the point of enrollment?
- Are families given information about local service agencies and the specific services provided?
- Is there a shared purpose and collaboration between the school district and community agencies to reduce the effects and frequency of student and family mobility within the larger community?

SERVICE OPPORTUNITIES

New families may also be eager to connect within the community as they establish new social and professional connections. They may have left communities where they were heavily involved in a variety of organizations, clubs, and churches, but now have no connections within the new environment.

This is another great opportunity for schools to serve as bridges to opportunities both within the school setting as well as to possibilities in the greater community.

- Are families given information about local volunteer opportunities and service organizations in the community?
- Is there a strong partnership established with community service organizations to provide outreach opportunities for new families?

Schools and school districts walk a fine line between providing community information to new families and serving as the local postal service for disseminating information. Having an effective system in place for receiving and distributing community information is an important factor for school districts as they help families connect with a variety of opportunities.

School district policies and procedures should be aligned to assure availability of resources as well as a process for dissemination.

Websites are also an important aspect of communication, and have become the primary source for many families and community agencies in terms of finding current information on events and activities. Many districts are effectively using social media for this purpose as well, and parents can sign up for services that provide an ongoing stream of information.

At the point of enrollment they may not be aware of the resources, therefore another step in planning is sharing those resources and possibly assisting in the set-up process. This is also true for helping parents and students gain access to district student information systems to view grades and information specific to classes and schedules at a specific school.

- Are families shown how to access school and district information on social media websites, school and district websites, and local media outlets such as radio and television stations?

ESSENTIAL IDEAS

- School and community connections are vital to helping families assimilate quickly and effectively into new environments.
- There are a variety of ways to make this happen, including involving local parent organizations and designating specific staff members for this purpose.
- Some of the most successful schools have other parents who are passionate about helping new families and students connect well and take specific steps to invite them to school activities and to connect with them at school events.
- Like the other steps in this book, the main focus is to make this a purposeful part of planning for effective transitions and should not be overlooked or seen as something outside the scope of the school.

TWELVE

The Ins and Outs of Exit Transitions

After multiple chapters dealing with helping mobile students enter a new place, it may seem rather contradictory to discuss aspects of sending them out again to yet another school on their educational journey.

Unfortunately, that is what high mobility is, and just as sure as students are going to come in the front doors, students are going to go out of them as well. The way schools assist in the exit process can help a student transition much more successfully in the next school if some attention is given to procedures that are used in the exit process.

INTERNAL MOBILITY

One problem many districts face with student mobility is movement within the school district, or intradistrict mobility. This type of mobility can be successfully derailed if students are allowed to remain at an attendance site, even if the home address is going to be outside of the designated attendance area.

However, the difficulty with this scenario is the issue of transportation and students arriving at school on time with consistency. When students are able to walk, they may be more likely to attend consistently if they are not dependent upon an undependable car or parent.

However, if districts can provide intradistrict transportation, every effort should be made to keep students at an attendance site whenever possible. Some districts have successfully established transportation routes within cities, including specific pick-up and drop-off points rather than a traditional door-to-door transportation model.

- Does the school district allow students to stay in the same school if they are living in a different attendance area?

- Does the district provide transportation options to help students stay in a school if it is outside of their attendance area?

CLOSURE

Some of the practices contained in this section may seem rather simple but are often overlooked. Classroom teachers may be aware that students are transitioning to another school; however; specialists and other support staff members may not realize they are leaving until after they are gone.

It is important to communicate information about student transitions to all staff in order to maintain the collective focus on helping all students make effective transitions both in and out of the school.

- Are practices in place to notify all staff members when new students arrive or when students are leaving?
- Are all staff members aware of the information they may be responsible for sharing when a student transitions to a new school?

CELEBRATE AND ACKNOWLEDGE

When significant time and effort have been invested in helping a student achieve new levels of success, there is a need for those who had a part in the process to celebrate, acknowledge, and enjoy some of the fruits of their labor as they send the child on to the next school.

If they are unable to acknowledge the positive effects of the work that has been done, there is a cumulative effect of feeling like the multiple efforts to help children may not matter and are not important.

The result is a fatigue factor that can lead to future apathy for helping mobile students and can easily be avoided if there is closure, recognition, and celebration.

- As students transition out of school, is academic progress reviewed and documented to share with the next receiving school?
- Are student achievements celebrated with the students and staff?

CLASSROOM CLOSURE

Classmates also need to be given the opportunity to say goodbye to students who leave and have some idea of where they are going to avoid the misconception that they somehow disappeared into thin air. Students often think they were expelled or gone for some other terrible reason other than the simple fact of moving.

This does not require a class party or other major event in the schedule, but does require the teacher to allow time for the student to tell their class they are leaving, and for classmates to say goodbye through simple notes, a classroom poster, or just verbally.

- Do students have a consistent opportunity to say goodbye to classmates when the teacher is aware of the move?

TRANSITIONING INFORMATION AND RECORDS

In order to help students transition to the new school, records and student information should be shared quickly and efficiently to create the best possible conditions for continuing learning right where it was left off, and for schools to have information for placement, meeting discipline problems proactively, and for helping families with specific needs.

All of these types of things can be done easily, but again, the practices must be purposeful to be consistent. When secretaries and school personnel become busy, these types of tasks may sit in a pile too long either on the sending or receiving end, and it is the student who suffers as a result.

- Does the school have specific practices for exiting students to other districts?
- Has an efficient method for transferring student records, such as electronic transfer or expedited mailings, been developed?
- Have forms been developed to assist in the efficient transfer of basic student information that would allow the new school to resume instruction at the correct level of difficulty?
- Do staff members know clearly what information can and should be shared, and the format for sharing it?

PARENT INFORMATION

One final component contained in the process of exiting students from a school is the need to share information about the effects of mobility directly with parents. Many parents are uneducated about the effects of mobility on student achievement, and while it may not deter their decisions to continue moving, it may at least cause them to think about it in a different way.

This also may reinforce the need for them to give better information during enrollment or help them to ask better questions when they arrive at the new school.

- Is information shared with families about the negative effects of mobility on student achievement?

- Is information shared with families about helping their child adjust to a new school?

The intent is not to make families feel guilty or ashamed for choosing to move again, but rather to educate them to at least allow for an informed decision. For a very few families, the information may actually influence the decision or at least the timing of a move and a child might endure one less transition.

ESSENTIAL IDEAS

- Schools would be remiss in allowing parents to continue to be uninformed about the effects of mobility.
- Information can be shared appropriately to help in the education process about the effects of high mobility and the impact on academic, social, and emotional development of a child.
- As students transition out of a school, additional steps can be put in place to give the students the best possible chance at their next school, and to model effective practices for schools that may not yet have them in place.

Whether it is a new form, a checklist, or a portfolio, essential information can be transferred to the next stop on the educational journey of a child.

THIRTEEN

Somebody Gets It—
Practical Application

Are there schools and administrators who understand the need for effective transition practices for mobile students? You bet! Not only do they understand the importance of effective practices, they have managed to keep entire schools focused on meeting the needs of mobile students.

They have managed to assemble entire teams of people from secretaries and custodians to classroom teachers and specialists, all who understand their roles in supporting mobile students as they enter and exit their schools.

Let us meet these people and find out what the driving forces are in helping students as they come and go, examining the specific characteristics of schools that get it, no matter if they are in large or small schools, rural or urban locations.

MEET FOUR ADMINISTRATORS

Jan is a female administrator from a large, urban district that has multiple resources to support the needs of mobile students. Her school has extended hours programs for students before school, after school, and during the summer months. She has many years of experience as an administrator and has made excellent use of financial and community resources. She has been at her school for over ten years.

Lou is a female administrator from a large school district in a rural location with some resources available to support the needs of mobile students. She demonstrates a high level of commitment to children of poverty and has many years of experience in education and at her school. She is highly committed to meeting the basic needs of children.

Jo is a female administrator from a small, rural district with fewer local resources to support the needs of mobile students. She has maximized the existing resources and has focused on a staff that is committed to meeting the needs of all children.

Pat is a male administrator in a mid-sized, rural district with strong after school programs. This district has a high level of community support and multiple programs in place to meet the needs of mobile students.

While the four administrators come from very different educational settings, critical components have been identified by all of them as being highly effective for mobility planning within the areas examined so far.

The specific components are listed in order to provide evidence of proven best practices in any environment.

ENROLLMENT BEST PRACTICES

Within the area of Enrollment Practices, the following items have been noted as being critically important to include as assurances within an effective Mobility Action Plan:

1. Identifying key adults in the school who are "first responders" for new families and students.
2. Creating a welcoming environment that includes a comfortable space for working on forms and one that does not interfere with the regular office or school routines.
3. Accessing multicultural liaisons to assist families whose primary language is not English in completing paperwork and answering questions at the time of enrollment.
4. Following a consistent plan for all students and families.
5. Having all introductory information and required paperwork ready to go ahead of time to expedite the enrollment process.
6. Counselors and secretaries are seen as critical leaders in connecting families with the new school.

ACADEMIC PLACEMENT BEST PRACTICES

Within the area of Academic Placement Practices, the following items are noted as being critically important to include as assurances within an effective Mobility Action Plan:

1. Academic pacing guides are part of the district curriculum planning structure.
2. Appropriate assessment is given in reading and math to determine classroom placements.

3. Teachers review practices on a yearly basis to make improvements and continue shared focus on appropriate placement for all students.

STUDENT PLACEMENT BEST PRACTICES

Within the area of Student Placement Practices, the following item is noted as being critically important to include as an assurance within an effective Mobility Action Plan:

1. Collective decisions are a critical part of effectively placing students in classrooms. In some places this is done formally as a team, and in other places the principal is the primary decision maker with input from other staff members.

CLASSROOM CONNECTION BEST PRACTICES

Within the area of Classroom Connection Practices, the following items are noted as being critically important to include as assurances within an effective Mobility Action Plan:

1. Classroom buddies are assigned to new students, and training is provided to all students in a volunteer role.
2. Students are consistently given building tours, orientations, and specific training on critical systems such as student discipline support plans.

FAMILY CONNECTIONS BEST PRACTICES

Within the area of Family Connections Practices, the following items are noted as being critically important to include as assurances within an effective Mobility Action Plan:

1. School staff members have had specific training related to the needs of families and students, such as understanding poverty as cultural proficiency.
2. Frequent opportunities are provided for parents to meet with each other and school officials to receive additional information and to provide feedback to the school.
3. Wraparound services are viewed as critical components for student and family well-being related to school.
4. Services and information are easily accessible, including onsite interpreters and translated materials for enrollment.

UNIQUE NEEDS BEST PRACTICES

Within the area of Unique Needs Practices, the following item is noted as being critically important to include as an assurance within an effective Mobility Action Plan:

1. Students are allowed to stay in the current school even if they move or are living outside of the school attendance area.

COMMUNITY CONNECTIONS BEST PRACTICES

Within the area of Community Connections Practices, the following items are noted as being critically important to include as assurances within an effective Mobility Action Plan:

1. Before and after school programs are offered for all students, with strong community partnerships to support ongoing funding and staffing needs.
2. Information is shared about community services including medical, social services, and spiritual support networks.
3. Summer programs are available for students, including family lunch services at multiple locations within the school district.

EXIT TRANSITIONS BEST PRACTICES

Within the area of Exit Transition Practices, the following items are noted as being critically important to include as assurances within an effective Mobility Action Plan:

1. Academic and behavioral plans are sent to the next school with specific information and progress reports.
2. Office staff have developed specific practices to expedite the transfer of records to provide the next school with timely and relevant information to assist with the transition into the new school.

VOICES FROM THE FIELD

All of the administrators agreed that the first critical piece of helping students and families transition effectively into a new school begins as they enter the building. Families must find a welcoming environment and be assisted by key people in the office such as a secretary or office aide whose primary responsibility is to welcome new families and assist them with registration procedures.

Pat's district had a centralized registration process, whereas the other schools registered students at the school. Pat stated in his building the secretary spends a lot of time with families and there is access to a bilingual paraprofessional.

"She goes through it (paperwork) and probably spends about an hour with every family and does a really, really thorough job in making them feel welcomed at our school, comfortable with the paperwork, and helps them if they need translators."

The administrators reiterated many times that phone conversations and initial contacts are critical to setting the stage for an entire positive school experience for new families.

—Jan's school used Title I funds specifically to hire someone in the office to help with families as they enrolled.

—"Our secretaries are the first people, they are our first welcome to anyone so they have to be people who have patience and time to make sure that everyone feels they are the most important thing they are doing."

Administrators were asked about practices involving other students in helping new students transition into their school. Jo and Lou's schools provide students with a tour of the building, conducted by other students when possible.

All of the schools have multiple services available for students, and include information about those programs in the practices of transitioning new families into the school community.

Many of the programs are based on poverty eligibility, and include things such as clothing banks, community learning centers, free food and vitamins for families, insurance for children, and services provided by various specialists including therapists and counselors. Jan stated, "I think the first connection is really important." At her school, students are partnered with a "buddy," and the counselor takes an active role in ongoing contact with the family to ensure a continued smooth transition.

—Pat's school assigns a student partner for a minimum of one week. The students are trained as "student ambassadors."

"We train a group of students specifically to be ambassadors so they learn some special techniques of helping students out and we try to encourage that child to stay with the newcomer, the new child for at least a full week."

In addition to providing students with partners and information about the basic routines and procedures in the school, Lou and Pat's schools provide additional training specific to the school discipline programs. The procedures include videos made by students to introduce new students to procedures and specific training from the school counselor.

All of the administrators take an active role themselves in meeting new families as part of the initial transition phase, and make sure to continue their contact with new students as they assimilate into their school. They encourage parents to seek them out with questions or problems and try to be very accessible and nonthreatening.

They also believe they help to set the tone of an inviting environment as people enter the school, and serve to establish a climate of welcoming families with their staff.

Lou stated, "I have had many people tell me that just as you enter the building, you can just feel this warmth that does not come from bricks and mortar. It comes from the people within the structure so I think that's first of all."

Jan referenced, "An amazing staff that reaches out and wants to build a partnership, wants to build a bond very quickly. I think that is our biggest asset."

Three of the schools have a one-day waiting period to start new students in order to allow teachers some time to prepare materials for them and to effectively introduce them into the classroom.

One of the schools saw the importance of routine and encouraged families to start students as soon as possible, even on the same day in order to get kids in school and minimize time missed by the transition to a new classroom. Lou's school took care to ask parents an extensive set of questions that would allow them to get information that would help with classroom placement.

"We question the parents on particulars within the family unit and we are able to make a more educated and informed decision about which classroom would be best for that child."

If parents have difficulty coming to the school, Jo's school offers to have services come to the home to facilitate the completion of paperwork and to accommodate the parent.

All of the schools obtain some sort of assessment data to use in placing students into classrooms, mainly in reading and math. Students who have English as a second language are also assessed to determine if any language support intervention services are needed.

GAINING FEEDBACK

One common theme was the importance of getting quality feedback from new families to make improvements or changes in practices and procedures. Two of the schools have specific procedures to follow up with parents at regular intervals following their registration to see if things are going smoothly and to answer any questions that might arise.

Jo stated that parents are surveyed each quarter in order to get ongoing feedback, and transition surveys are given specifically to sixth grade and ninth grade students as they moved from elementary to junior high and then from junior high to high school to gauge the effectiveness of those changes.

Jan's school has parent groups that meet on a weekly basis, which is also the time that the school counselor and social workers are available specifically to meet with families.

"She (counselor) has just been able to connect with parents in ways that you could just hope would happen in your school," Lou said.

Pat's district uses study circles to meet the specific needs of parents and to help them understand more about what their children are learning in school. Schedules have been adjusted to accommodate parent work schedules to allow for increased participation.

EVERYONE IS WELCOME

Administrators could identify specific practices put in place to help new families feel welcome when they come to a new school.

At conferences, multicultural liaisons are available to answer questions in a parent's first language. This is common to the three districts of Jan, Lou, and Pat that have students who speak a first language other than English.

All have services available at the school or within the district to meet the communication needs of non-English speaking parents. Having a bilingual staff person is seen as beneficial by all of the schools with ELL families. This allows families to make an immediate connection to the school in a comfortable way and to have a person they identify as being "safe" or approachable.

Jo's district provides a nonthreatening environment with a strong focus on helping parents with paperwork, and working with parents to get required documentation for students in order to allow them to start school. She states there is an emphasis on building trust with parents and students, and her district even provides services in the home to assist parents in completing necessary paperwork.

CONSISTENCY IS THE KEY

All of the administrators indicated that consistent information is shared and standard forms are used to obtain information from families. Lou focused on specific procedures followed such as building tours, meeting the principal, and having meetings with the school counselor as part of an intake system.

Lou stated that practices and procedures have been articulated more clearly as a result of their Title I Peer Review during the previous school year.

All schools have materials available and ready for families and know specifically which staff members are responsible for specific tasks and obtaining relevant information from families.

In the four represented districts, students are allowed to stay in their school whenever possible if they move out of an attendance area. However, many parents opt to move students to a school closer to a new home due to transportation or daycare needs.

Lou said, "We have a process in place that is very formalized and it is done in a very collaborative fashion so we are sure every student is assigned as much as possible and we're meeting the requests of the parents. They are moving for any number of reasons and we're able to allow them the opportunity to stay at their school."

For Jo's district, students are able to progress from their present instructional level and modifications are made for appropriate placement and interventions. She stated she often forgets what grade students are in because of the large amount of cross-grade level grouping that occurs to meet the academic needs of individual students.

ONGOING ACADEMIC OPPORTUNITIES

All four districts offer before and/or after school programming needs to meet the academic needs of students, and to lessen the effects of mobility on achievement scores. Multiple programs exist, including tutoring, homework help, extra learning time, volunteers who read with students, and enrichment classes or clubs.

Summer programs are also offered in all districts. One of the hallmarks of schools with mobile students is that services for students do not begin and end with a bell. They extend throughout the day and into the evening, on weekends, and over the summer with a large number of families taking advantage of the services.

It is evident that there is a strong commitment on the part of staff when practices are put into action to meet the needs of students.

Lou said that empathy was a big part of their staff commitment. "I think that just the empathy piece is very critical and my staff is always looking for ways to do wraparound services for kids. Working in a Title I school, if you're really doing what's right for kids, is very difficult work."

At Lou's school, students participate in a catch-up lab if they have been absent in order to complete missed work.

At Jan's school, both remedial and accelerated programs are offered for students. Remedial programs were in place to help students acquire skills that have not been mastered while accelerated programs are designed to give students a head start on learning what is to come the following year.

Instructional materials are also a factor in reducing the effects of mobility on academic achievement. Programs that offer multiple instructional group settings are common as well as programs that provide continual review of material while moving students ahead with new concepts.

Lou stated that quick and easy assessments provide valuable data for determining the skill levels of new students and allow them to begin services with appropriate interventions.

Pat's school has a heavy focus on tutoring that is available before and after school. This type of intervention has proven successful for many of the highly mobile students. The success of many of the existing district programs is due to strong community partnerships such as a YMCA or other community centers.

INSTRUCTIONAL CONSISTENCY

The issue of consistency is a common concern for district-wide expectations for pacing and instructional guides. The districts of the administrators follow district expectations for pacing, and teachers have a clear understanding of where they are to be on a schedule both quarterly, and in some cases, on a daily or weekly basis.

These kinds of initiatives have been developed specifically for the purpose of addressing intradistrict mobility.

Pat's school district operates on quarterly expectations for pacing and assessment. In Lou's district, pacing guides were developed specifically for the purpose of minimizing the effects of mobility within the district. Teachers were involved in the process of developing the guides.

Jo's district operates on quarterly expectations; however in the area of reading, pacing is regulated almost on a daily basis. Jan's school district also has pacing guides that are followed by the week, but still noted the problem of missing instruction with students coming from other outside districts.

TEACHER ATTITUDES

Administrators from all of the schools praised their staff for having positive attitudes toward student mobility, and staff have received training specific for meeting the needs of students and families from a poverty background. Jan stated that staff members have a single focus.

"Their job is to build a community of learners. Their job is to make sure everyone is included and welcomed and loved."

Lou said, "We have an incredible staff who really care about kids and sometimes that human aspect comes through but then they get right back on the horse and ride it until it drops."

All principals acknowledged the fact that it is difficult for teachers to have continual movement of students into and out of the classroom, and it is discouraging at times because of the investment they make in each individual child. Jo said that even though they have more mobility than ever before, she is proud of the way the teachers and the staff step up to meet the needs of students.

"I have never seen anyone roll their eyes and say I do not want that kid." She went on to say the only frustration that often surfaces is the teacher wanting to make sure they do the best possible job for the student, given the fact that they have multiple areas of deficit and obvious gaps in their learning.

Pat spoke of the collegial nature of the teachers and said, "We just really work to support one another and our teachers have a great attitude. It just happens so frequently, it is just so much a way that we do business. I just do not see any negativity related to that even late in the year."

Jan's teachers take an active role in how mobility affects their classrooms by being the main facilitators of placement decisions for students. Teams make decisions based on what they think is best for the child after they have been given various pieces of academic and behavioral information.

Lou spoke about the needs of students arising from generational poverty that often results in a high degree of mobility and the frustration that causes for teachers. "That's one of the things I talk about with the teachers all the time that our work here is so critical because our children's needs are not being met. We put together a curriculum of care that is very direct and very specific because frankly we do not have time to undo all of the damage that has occurred."

FINAL THOUGHTS IN THEIR OWN WORDS—LOU

I think the most important thing is to have a solid protocol for orientation into your building to make people see this is a welcoming place and that we have practices in place that are going to help your child feel more comfortable and that this is a place where they can feel at home.

I think number two that is critical is the suspension of judgment. People will just open up their heart if they believe that you really want to genuinely help their child. I guess I would say hire people who genuinely can put themselves out there for families because families can spot a phony in a minute and they know if you do not mean it.

The third thing is to have some strong modeling and supports in place so when families say we do not have a quiet place for our children to work, and then we can say gosh we have all those things that are going to help you. We have some very specific things in place to help address needs so parents cannot use the excuse that I do not have what it takes and neither does the school.

We have some very specific things in place and sometimes we have to mandate those things for kids but for the most part people see very, very quickly that we are not going to let children fail here. Failure is not an option and we've got things in place that are going to help put some punch to that because to say that is easy but to actualize and formalize it so that it is part of your culture, that's the difficult part.

I think to summarize everything that I have said, this is the best job I have ever had and I feel missionary zeal for this work and I think if you do not feel missionary zeal it is really hard to do this work because it is so much more than you ever learned in any program in college.

You cannot teach someone to be a nurturing, caring person and at the same time be focused and purposeful. That is part of who you are and I think you have to hire people to staff schools that have high mobility rates and that have high poverty rates with people who have a genuine care about children and about making the lives of the children of America better.

I want to be in a school where families need me and I can work hard for kids and if someone wants to call me a bulldog for kids, boy what a compliment that is!

FINAL THOUGHTS IN THEIR OWN WORDS — JO

You need to recognize it is not the child's fault. They're victims of where their parents are going. Their parents may be just simply trying to make a living. I guess you know that goes without saying that should be the "aha" moment of understanding. But kids do not choose where they go, so to me it is like why would you ever? If they have a file this thick, if nothing else, you should see and recognize that the kid needs so much more support.

Get parents on your side as soon as you can. I think one of the most difficult things coming into this community is finding a network of support. Sometimes people aren't comfortable going to churches. You assume that would be a place people would go, but not necessarily so.

Sometimes parents are not comfortable in schools so you need to look at different places where you can offer a more nonthreatening environment. I think it is all about community connections. If you have highly mobile kids, I think you'd better be connecting with your community. Places where people can go and build positive relationships and good things are happening.

FINAL THOUGHTS IN THEIR OWN WORDS — PAT

I think it is really important not to be afraid of the families. Everything will take more time and almost everything needs to be face-to-face communication. What I always tell my teachers is come to every situation with an open heart, an open mind, and seek first to understand, then to be understood.

I would encourage schools to definitely find the resources to employ translators and interpreters and put in place some specific things just for communicating with parents. And recognize they have to meet them where they are and honor what they know. They're very perceptive and they know whether you love their children or not.

If you can just share with the rest of the world not to be afraid of this (diverse population). I really enjoy working with our community, our immigrant population. We also have tremendous support in our community. People have been willing to solve problems and not just blame.

FINAL THOUGHTS IN THEIR OWN WORDS—JAN

You have to have a first person they meet. It is the key. Make sure you have someone there that understands what teachers need, understands what we have to offer a family, and can be welcoming and helpful. The sooner you have the information you need, the better you can start serving that child and that family.

ESSENTIAL IDEAS

- Whether a mobile student is enrolling in an elementary school, a middle school, or a high school, relationships are clearly at the center of any effective practices that can be implemented.
- Staff members must share a collective vision that has at the core a strong desire to do the right thing for people, regardless of their circumstances.
- All of the best practices in the world will not be effective unless the central aim is to serve others.

FOURTEEN
Legal Complexities

Transitions to new schools are complex and difficult, but there are often extenuating circumstances that can make the move even more complex. These circumstances should be considered when looking through the wider lens of student mobility and effective transitions for families.

While not always pleasant, realities influence multiple aspects of the transition process, including student enrollment, attendance, and student information.

CUSTODY ISSUES

When parents arrive at a new school to enroll students, it is assumed they are the legal parent or guardian. However, most schools have experienced multiple issues related to legal custody and guardianship. One parent may have primary custody and does not want the noncustodial parent to have access to the student or students.

Unless parental rights have been terminated, the noncustodial parent still has the right to be involved in the child's school activities and is entitled to related information.

Issues also can arise from joint custody arrangements when one parent decides to leave the current location and enroll the child in another school district without informing the other parent. The other parent may object, and the school finds itself directly in the middle of a heated battle for control over the school setting of the child. This may be part of the reason for the transition occurring in the first place.

Finally, issues can erupt when non-spouses of the parents are involved by being listed as emergency contacts or as people who are allowed to pick up the child from school. When custody battles take place, these people are often part of the arguments that ensue when situations happen such as the father's girlfriend picking up the child when the mother shows up and protests, stating she has not given permission for that person to transport her child.

It is important to have great clarity of information during the enrollment process if parents are divorced or separated, and if there are battles being waged where the child is caught in the middle of frequent disputes. Disruptions can occur on school grounds, and school personnel should always reserve the right to call law enforcement when assistance is needed.

It is also critically important to obtain relevant legal documentation that specifically informs custody arrangements and visitation stipulations. If there are questions about parental rights or specific items contained in the documents, legal counsel should be sought on behalf of the school and school district to ensure correct legal interpretation.

DOMESTIC VIOLENCE, SHELTERS, AND THE HOMELESS

Part of the enrollment process requires information about the home address of the child. However, there are times when families may be displaced due to situations stemming from domestic violence or abuse in the home, and students are living temporarily in a local shelter or with a friend or relative. In this case, the home address may be temporary at best, or may be easily identifiable by office staff as a location for the homeless.

Schools must be sensitive to families in crisis situations, allowing some measure of privacy, while still obtaining adequate information about the student and fulfilling the legal requirements for enrollment. Staff members must be skilled at discerning when this is the case, and provide an extra measure of care and sensitivity, knowing families may be embarrassed, fearful, or nervous at the point when they arrive at school and are asked to provide the information.

Depending on the school, this may not be an uncommon occurrence, but in places where it occurs more infrequently, practices should be reviewed to accommodate this type of need. Students may have left their previous location without many clothes or basic school supplies.

Schools can be ready to assist with immediate needs by having supplies on hand, including backpacks, coats, and other basic clothing articles. Students may already feel isolated or anxious for fear of appearing "different" from their peers, and basic school supplies can make all the difference.

Many community partners are more than willing to help schools with this type of need, and can directly impact the well-being of students. In some school districts, every school has a community partner that offers support for mobile students and students living in poverty. This is a tremendously valuable type of partnership, and one that should be nurtured over time.

SEX OFFENDER REGISTRY

In most states, registered sex offenders are required to report their status to schools and local law enforcement agencies, and abide by state laws that govern school district policies. At the very least, this presents an awkward situation for the parent in this situation when the information is shared, and can also create fear or apprehension for the school community, depending on the nature of the offense that led to the legal designation.

Some parents may choose to share additional information while others may not, and depending on the state, varying degrees of information can be obtained from a public registry source. Most questions will center on the parent's ability to transport a child to and from school, or how to obtain permission to attend school events and activities.

A related situation can occur when information from another source is shared with the school regarding a registered sex offender, but the person required to share that information has chosen not to do so. At that point, the school must follow up but should do so carefully and with some guidance from legal counsel.

Laws vary from state to state, and policies differ from district to district. For the purposes of enrollment and transition, school staff should be aware of this possibility and ready to respond with respect for the person within the context of legal requirements.

ILLEGAL IMMIGRANT STATUS

Children in the United States are entitled to a free and appropriate education. Districts may require a birth certificate for a child but may not require a social security number. Districts may not deny enrollment if a child has a foreign birth certificate or if a family does not provide a social security number.

A number of federal statutes specifically prohibit discrimination practices that discourage participation or lead to exclusion from school based on parents' or guardians' actual or perceived citizenship or immigration status.

This may be a factor in the mobility rate of some students but should not create further barriers for the enrollment process. Training for staff should include a component of dealing with related issues and should contain clear guidelines that are aligned with federal and state immigration laws.

Measures should also be taken to reduce the amount of fear and anxiety the enrollment process may create for families that may already be somewhat afraid of forms and people in authority. Staff members should be extremely aware of their own behavior and demeanor so a new parent does not experience any undue fear or intimidation.

Even though schools are largely viewed as happy, welcoming places, the actual office itself can create some apprehension for visitors. Expectations for a positive transition experience for all students and families should be the central focus when faced with this type of scenario.

MEDIA RELEASE—SOME RESTRICTIONS APPLY

Most enrollment forms contain some type of indicator for granting permission to publish a child's photo or routine directory information. Schools must have systems that allow for easy access to the information in order to ensure appropriate checks are conducted when needed.

When a parent does not allow this information to be released, including photos of a child, it may be due to some of the situations listed in this chapter. This is a step that can be easily overlooked unless there is a designated staff member who assures this takes place consistently.

Schools must take extra care to know and implement all district policies and state legal requirements surrounding this type of student privacy issue.

LAWSUITS AND ANTAGONISTS

Unfortunately, frequent transitions can stem from ugly legal situations where families move out of necessity for safety or due to outcomes mandated by the courts. Legal custody can change due to abuse, divorce, or removal from the home.

If there are ongoing legal issues, parents may become antagonistic toward the school or staff members as part of an effort to prove requirements are not being met or to place blame on the other parent or the school.

Parents may be antagonistic when requesting documentation, involving the school in court appearances or depositions, or during unplanned visits to the school. Any number of situations may arise, from unfriendly altercations in the parking lot to physical removal by law enforcement.

With a growing emphasis on school safety and security, schools must stay alert to this kind of information if it is shared during the enrollment process or thereafter. Effective communication is vital when a parent or guardian presents a potential threat to school safety. Information can be shared discreetly in order to respect the privacy of the family, but effectively to ensure the safety of staff and students.

This scenario typically manifests itself when a noncustodial parent threatens to remove a child against court orders, or when a distraught parent tries to gain access to a child through the doors of the school. Domestic violence can also be a very real factor related to any number of situations, and schools are easy targets with predictable schedules and relatively easy access for entry.

ESSENTIAL IDEAS

- The complexities of the family dynamics mentioned in this chapter should never be overlooked within the context of enrollment and student mobility.
- Effective practices should be viewed through a wide lens of related complex issues that can directly affect students in transition, even resulting in harmful circumstances.
- Legal considerations require the assistance of experts who can offer specific guidance for difficult issues and situations.
- It is important to understand that many planned and unplanned moves are the direct result of life situations well outside of the control of children.
- Schools are often the most stable places in the lives of students and great care should be given to maintaining that position.

FIFTEEN

A Call to Action

Words that come to mind when reviewing the best practices are commitment, community, connections, communication, care, and concern. Procedures can be implemented and put into place, but unless a committed staff creates a climate of care and concern, follows through with involving the community through partnerships and support, and communicates effectively with families, the results will be minimal, even if a written transition plan exists.

Common threads emerge in buildings including a climate of care that exists within each school and among staff members. There is an ongoing effort of cultivation and putting into practice the art of doing whatever it takes. It is the actual doing, not talking about doing, but digging in one's heels in terms of time, resources, creativity, volunteering, partnering, and getting things done for children.

Schools have to quit bemoaning the problem and begin taking steps to solve the problem. This begins from the inside out and requires both a shift in the climate and culture of the school as well as effective implementation of steps in multiple areas that address the needs of highly mobile students.

Students are not in control of their mobility, but we as educators are in control of how needs are met for any student who walks through the doors, regardless of the reasons why.

When multiple practices are consistently in place, staff members are committed and existing resources are well utilized. Successful transitions can result for mobile students throughout the school year.

FOCUS ON SOLUTIONS

The right steps to take are clearly laid out within the chapter categories, the focus questions, the real life examples, and verbal pictures taken straight from places where effective and consistent practices are well established.

So what will schools do?

When the next student walks in to register at your school, are you willing to tell them they are the one who is not going to have friends ready to meet them in their new classroom?

Are you willing to explain to a parent why you cannot immediately provide reading services to a struggling reader?

Are you ready to deal with the behavior problems that might be part of a student's needs because a parent fails to tell you they have been on a strict behavior plan and are taking high doses of antipsychotic medication?

It is simply no longer acceptable to let any child fail as a result of transition practices that could have been put in place but instead were ignored or delayed. It is not good enough to wait for the sending school to send information and records that are incomplete, delayed, or simply nonexistent. We can no longer rely on every parent who comes to register a child to provide usable and accurate information to appropriately serve the child's needs.

The time to take action is now. As schools develop plans to meet the needs of students, those ideas and initiatives will grow and travel to other schools, creating a cycle of ongoing improvements in the area of successful transitions for mobile students. Let us together start the process of expecting all schools to implement these practices, for all students, in every district, every time.

As you begin to use the results of this book to shape your plan, bring everyone to the table. Everyone has a role in helping students make successful transitions, but they need to know what that role is.

Secretaries and paraprofessionals need to know exactly for which practices they are responsible in the office from the moment the paperwork is started to the point that the child enters the door. Practices should be followed with fidelity to ensure newcomers have the same quality experience whether they come in August or April.

School nurses need to know their role in sorting out the health needs of a new student, and can expedite services and plans as quickly as possible. They need to understand that their role is critical to the well-being of the child as a learner in the classroom they enter.

Counselors, social workers, and psychologists are the first line of responders in connecting with students and offer a wealth of expertise and practical ideas for schools.

Food service and maintenance staff members need to understand how they play a part in welcoming new students, and have to be aware of the students who are entering the building. They are the front lines for managing food allergies and dietary restrictions. They need to know the name that goes with the new face when students come through the line for their first school lunch.

Specialists need to be aware of new students coming to the school so they can be ready as they enter the classroom. How many students have heard a specialist say to a classroom teacher, "I didn't know you got a new student. I do not have a book for them yet." Or how about, "We're getting ready for our concert so they'll have to sit over there since they do not know the music."

Specialists are critical players in welcoming new students but are often left out of the information and accountability loop when making transition plans.

All teachers, whether in the regular education or special education setting, deserve to know when new students are enrolled in the school. Not only is it important if the teacher will teach the student directly, but also to build a shared vision and purpose for everyone working in the school.

A spirit of collective community and care has to envelop new students if they are to sense a strong welcome at every turn in their new school.

Most importantly, students in every class need to know and understand their role in helping new students as they enter the classroom. They need to build a sense of empathy and understanding for how the experience is shaped for another person by their actions.

They need to also understand that everyone comes to a classroom with a different picture. If they have started their picture at that school, they have a shared idea of what school is. But students coming from other places have other parts to their picture that have to be blended with the new school environment.

Children need to see how their own experience can be enriched by the influence of a new student as well as how their experience shapes that of the new student. If a reciprocal kind of structure can be achieved, students no longer see the transition as a disruption or opportunity to reestablish the pecking order.

Rather they can begin to see it as a blending and sharing type of scenario, and some of the potential conflicts that can arise might be diminished or removed altogether. Bullying can be reduced when students see their collective influence on the positive climate and culture of their school.

No matter where you find yourself within the school calendar, it is never the wrong time to develop and implement a solid Mobility Action Plan. This is not something that can wait until another new year rolls around, and the enrollment process begins again.

It does not take a long, cumbersome process with multiple committee meetings and lengthy action plans. It takes the realization that students deserve the best we can offer, the commitment to quality over time, and the shared vision to make the process of transition a positive experience for all mobile students and families as they come to your school.

Students are largely not in control of the moves they experience. Begin using these tools today to influence the transition process for every new student that walks in the door.

Appendix A: Questions by Chapter

This section contains the sequential questions beginning in chapter 5. Answers can be recorded here to capture responses individually or collectively. After the questions have been completed, use the information to begin crafting an effective Mobility Action Plan.

CHAPTER 5

1. Is visitor parking readily available and identified for people visiting the school?
2. If the office is not located near the main entrance of the school, are there clear directions that visibly guide people to the right location?
3. Are classroom teachers and support staff as eager to meet students in the middle of the year as they were during the scheduled Open House?
4. Do the right faces belong to the first faces?
5. Are there specific staff members who are designated to carry out the procedures?
6. Can all staff members clearly articulate their role in the enrollment process?
7. After the initial start of the year, are the enrollment forms still easily accessible?
8. Is there a comfortable place to complete forms and ask questions?
9. Is all relevant information for new students and families easily accessible through the school website?
10. Are families given a complete list of supplies students need to begin school?
11. If supplies are unavailable or unobtainable, does the school provide them?
12. Are translated materials or the services of a translator available as needed?
13. If a translator is not available on site, are there clear procedures for contacting one?
14. Are staff members culturally proficient when a variety of cultures are represented in the community?

15. Do families receive written and verbal information about school procedures?
16. Are materials simple and easy to read?
17. Are parents asked to pay additional fees when enrolling in school that might be unexpected?
18. Is information regarding fee waivers available at the time of enrollment?
19. Do families receive written and verbal information about school procedures?
20. Are materials simple and easy to read with an average readability at or below eighth grade?
21. Are consistent procedures followed for enrolling all new students?
22. Are school tours provided for all new students and families?
23. Are families given clear information about how to contact the school office?
24. Do enrollment forms and communication tools reflect options or information that encompasses diverse family structures?
25. Are systems in place for notifying existing staff members and students when new students arrive?
26. Is the classroom or homeroom teacher personally introduced to the new student and family?

CHAPTER 5 REFLECTION

Based on your responses and discussion, what are the current areas of strength in your school?
What areas need to be developed more completely?
What specific action steps need to be included in your School Mobility Plan?

CHAPTER 6

1. Are requests for student records or new files processed in a short amount of time?
2. Have adequate processes been put in place to assure records are not delayed in the sending or receiving of information?
3. Do office staff members understand the importance of student file information in reviewing academic, social, and attendance data for new students?
4. Does the information sent from your school contain information that makes subsequent placements easier for receiving schools?

5. Are there designated assessments used for the specific purposes of placing a student based on academic needs?
6. Are specific assessments given to determine a student's current reading level?
7. Are specific assessments given to determine a student's current math level?
8. Can specialists such as reading teachers or ELL teachers take the data and quickly design a plan that is targeted directly at the most critical areas of learning?
9. Are the needs of the student specifically matched to the strengths of the classroom teacher?

CHAPTER 6 REFLECTION

Based on your responses and discussion, what are the current areas of strength in your school?

What areas need to be developed more completely?

What specific action steps need to be included in your School Mobility Plan?

CHAPTER 7

1. Are placement decisions based heavily on gender balance?
2. Does a team of people have input on placement decisions or is it isolated to one person?
3. Are placement decisions based heavily on racial balance?
4. Is there a lack of racial balance because of scheduling and services?
5. Have other creative measures been considered to provide viable alternatives for services?
6. Have questions been developed as part of the enrollment process, specific to supplemental or primary services such as special education, ELL, gifted, or intervention services if educational records are unavailable?
7. Are people willing to serve on a school enrollment team?
8. Are the unique characteristics and expertise needed for the enrollment team identified for your school?

CHAPTER 7 REFLECTION

Based on your responses and discussion, what are the current areas of
   strength in your school?
What areas need to be developed more completely?
What specific action steps need to be included in your School Mobility
   Plan?

CHAPTER 8

1. Are all students assigned a peer buddy that has been trained for
   this role?
2. Are non-English speaking students assigned a peer buddy who
   speaks their home language?
3. Are a variety of students trained to be buddies in order to match
   new students based on common interest and personalities?
4. Are there consistent practices in place that guide the student orientation process in every classroom?
5. Are classroom teachers trained in specific strategies focused on
   receiving new students in their class and in the school?
6. Are students introduced to other teachers they may have during
   the course of their day?
7. Do students have an opportunity to share personal information
   with all teachers who are part of their daily schedule?
8. Are students assigned to an adult mentor other than the classroom
   teacher?
9. Are all students given a tour of the school when they arrive no
   matter when they arrive during the day or during the school year?
10. Do all students have a school orientation to learn procedures for
    areas outside of their classroom, such as the lunchroom, play-
    ground, or media center?
11. Do students know emergency procedures such as evacuation
    drills?
12. Do students know expectations for secured entrances and exits
    such as not opening doors for adults who are waiting to enter?
13. Do parents of new students know school procedures and expecta-
    tions for safety and security measures?

CHAPTER 8 REFLECTION

Based on your responses and discussion, what are the current areas of strength in your school?

What areas need to be developed more completely?

What specific action steps need to be included in your School Mobility Plan?

CHAPTER 9

1. Have staff members been designated to serve as point people for new families when they come to the school to enroll?
2. Have schedules been reviewed to provide the best coverage possible for welcoming families at any point in the school day?
3. Are families given an orientation that covers both academic and nonacademic information?
4. Are parents aware of the learning expectations for the grade level of their child?
5. Are parents informed about the educational intervention and extension opportunities available for their child?
6. Is technology being leveraged as a tool to provide information and opportunities for parents and families?
7. Is the information provided through school and district websites up-to-date and accurate?
8. Is a parent from the school who is identified as a family liaison available to contact new families?
9. Are new families specifically invited to attend school events?
10. Are families encouraged to volunteer at school by providing a written list of volunteer opportunities?
11. Does the school administrator or other staff member contact new families to help with the transition?

CHAPTER 9 REFLECTION

Based on your responses and discussion, what are the current areas of strength in your school?

What areas need to be developed more completely?

What specific action steps need to be included in your School Mobility Plan?

CHAPTER 10

1. Are student health needs communicated to the school health office and classroom teacher upon enrollment?
2. Are other staff members notified about health needs relevant to their assignments?
3. Do parents know how to reach the school office and health professionals, and do they know the plan in place for their child's needs?
4. Does the school have an interpreter on staff that can accommodate the needs of the students during the school day?
5. If an interpreter is not readily available, can other accommodations be made to meet the needs of the child until one can be obtained?
6. Is basic information shared with all relevant staff members in order to facilitate appropriate accommodations in multiple classrooms for new students?
7. Is there a process in place for noting and providing for specific physical accommodations that may be necessary for new students?
8. Are processes in place for making accommodations quickly and efficiently such as Student Assistance Teams or Response to Intervention protocols?

CHAPTER 10 REFLECTION

Based on your responses and discussion, what are the current areas of strength in your school?
What areas need to be developed more completely?
What specific action steps need to be included in your School Mobility Plan?

CHAPTER 11

1. Are materials about the community made available to new families at the point of enrollment?
2. Are families given information about local service agencies and the services provided?
3. Is there a shared purpose and collaboration between the school district and community agencies to reduce the effects and frequency of student and family mobility within the larger community?
4. Are families given information about local volunteer opportunities and service organizations in the community?

5. Is there a strong partnership established with community service organizations to provide outreach opportunities for new families?
6. Are families shown how to access school and district information on social media websites, school and district websites, and local media outlets such as radio and television stations?

CHAPTER 11 REFLECTION

Based on your responses and discussion, what are the current areas of strength in your school?

What areas need to be developed more completely?

What specific action steps need to be included in your School Mobility Plan?

CHAPTER 12

1. Does the school district allow students to stay in the same school if they are living in a different attendance area?
2. Does the district provide transportation options to help students stay in a school if it is outside of their attendance area?
3. Are practices in place to notify all staff members when new students arrive or when students are leaving?
4. Do staff members know clearly what information can and should be shared, and the format for sharing it?
5. As students transition out of school, is academic progress reviewed and documented to share with the next receiving school?
6. Are student achievements celebrated with the students and staff?
7. Do students have a consistent opportunity to say goodbye to classmates when the teacher is aware of the move?
8. Does the school have specific practices for exiting students to other districts?
9. Has an efficient method for transferring student records, such as electronic transfer or expedited mailings, been developed?
10. Have forms been developed to assist in the efficient transfer of basic student information that would allow the new school to resume instruction at the correct level of difficulty?
11. Do staff members know clearly what information can and should be shared, and the format for sharing it?
12. Is information shared with families about the negative effects of mobility on student achievement?

13. Is information shared with families about helping their child adjust to a new school?

CHAPTER 12 REFLECTION

Based on your responses and discussion, what are the current areas of strength in your school?

What areas need to be developed more completely?

What specific action steps need to be included in your School Mobility Plan?

Appendix B: Scenarios for Group Discussion and Interaction

Scenarios

The following scenarios are based on real situations of student mobility. Use the vignettes to facilitate discussions around the steps that could be taken to support the students and families in the scenarios. Look for similarities and differences in the students served at your school to think about your current practices and ways you can improve. Remember how important the experience of transitions is for every student, every family, every time they are in the care of your school or district.

SCENARIO #1

I remember very little about the classrooms I was placed in during my elementary years. I remember how relieved I would be when the class was covering something I had already learned at another school because I could raise my hand and display my superior knowledge. But at other times I would feel so far out of the loop from what students were learning or the projects that were often underway that I would retreat to a book and hope my teacher would leave me alone. My teachers were always somewhat surprised when they found out I was a good reader. They would often start me in the low group, but quickly figure out that I was a high flyer when it came to reading. You see, no matter what town we were in, libraries always had free books and that was one thing my mother always made sure of — that we knew where the library was and that we had a library card. That left more "free time" for her and her guests when we were allowed to spend the afternoon immersed in our books or enjoying the activities at the local library.

"Terry" — Mobile student in the 1980s

SCENARIO #2

I knew it. We had another new student enrolled and they were placed in my class due to my "expertise" at handling severe behavior needs. I admit I have done extensive training and I really do understand these children better than some of my colleagues, but does that mean I should be penalized and worn to a frazzle because I can handle it? My principal has no idea how exhausted I am when I get home, and how mad my husband is at me when I am distracted or mentally spent—too much so to go out with him for a meal or for a family activity. Many days I feel like I'm purely in survival mode and am virtually ignoring the rest of my "normal" students. It is easy to say that kids are resilient and can be successful with a variety of needs present in the classroom, but when students kick, hit, bite, spit, and throw things at you, you begin to wonder if teaching is really worth it, or if it would be better for everyone to find another job!

"Sharon" — Teacher in a high mobility school

SCENARIO #3

I had to go to the bathroom all morning, but I was not getting out of my seat. I didn't know where the outhouse was, and I was not going by myself. I was also hungry, but I was too scared to eat, so my lunch sat on the back shelf and I took it home with me. My mother asked me why I didn't eat anything and I started to cry. I had spent the entire day not knowing any of the language my teacher spoke, not knowing any of the students, and wondering why I had to go to school at all. I did not like this new place called school, and I didn't see why I would have to leave my mother and grandmother to go there again the next day.

"Donna" — One-room schoolhouse ELL student from Sweden in the 1930s

SCENARIO #4

Pam was homeless and the mother of four children. When she walked into the school to register her children, no one looked up. The secretary was on the phone, there was confusion in the office, and they seemed to be just another family waiting for someone to notice.

The secretary finished her call and looked up without smiling, and curtly asked if she could help. Behind her words Pam quickly picked up on the feeling that she was hoping they were not there to enroll more children. It seemed that the last thing this school wanted was to see more children.

Pam was given a clipboard full of papers, a pencil that needed to be sharpened, and was sent to a table out in the hallway where everyone walking by could size things up. She struggled to keep the younger children quiet and close as she worked her way through yet another set of forms. She was getting good at them, but they still took a lot of time.

After she was finished, she walked back in and was told her children could start the next day if she could produce their birth certificates and immunization records. She had hoped the copies of those documents would have arrived with the information from their last school, but she was wrong. Maybe somewhere in the sacks buried in the trunk of her car she would be able to find those magic documents by morning.

"Pam" — Battered mother of four staying at the shelter

SCENARIO #5

John came from a highly abusive home. He knew his mother did the best she could for their family, but they were a rough and rowdy bunch and on the move a lot as a result. They lived in eleven or twelve different towns by the time John was in high school, so when he is asked where he is from, he does not really have an answer.

His brothers were known to really behave badly, so when they would move and start to get in trouble, John's teachers naturally assumed that he was made of the same stuff. Whenever something happened in the classroom, it was often assumed that John had something to do with it. He spent a fair share of time in the principal's office or being suspended, usually with very little evidence that he was actually involved.

In high school, John's wrestling coach saw some potential in his athletic skills and got to know him as a person, which was extremely rare for him at this point. One day his coach said, "You know, you do not have to grow up to be like them."

John knew at that moment his coach saw something different, and as a result, he saw something different for himself as well. Hope.

"John" — Mobile student in a rural setting

SCENARIO #6

Ben and his family entered their new high school accompanied by the bilingual assistant from the district office. As they entered school, everything felt unfamiliar from sights and sounds, to the long, brick hallway. They were new to this school, new to the state, and new to the country.

As they walked into the office, they were handed a set of forms translated into their own language. The liaison was able to translate the information verbally, but neither Ben nor his parents were able to read the writing on the forms.

When asked his age, Ben said seventeen. That meant technically, Ben should be placed in a junior or senior class. Transcripts were not available for Ben because he had fled his country along with his family, with very few belongings and no ability to contact the school he had attended.

The counselors and registrar would need to figure out the appropriate placement for Ben, develop a schedule that would help him learn English, and keep him on target to graduate with his peers. No transcript, no birth certificate, and no English.

"Ben" — An ELL high school student

Appendix C: Mobility Action Plan Framework

School Name
Mobility Action Plan—Framework

If your school has a collective mission, vision, or belief statement about your commitment to serving mobile students and families, insert that as part of your plan.

GETTING STARTED—FORMING THE ACTION PLAN

1. Under each heading below, list the specific action steps generated from the questions in each chapter to meet the needs of your school.
2. After action steps have been identified and defined, begin looking at the people who are attached to those action steps to determine and clarify roles and responsibilities.
3. As people are identified for roles and responsibilities, analyze those choices related to the daily schedule to determine where there may be gaps or overlaps in availability of staff members to cover an assigned responsibility.

Enrollment
Academic Placement
Student Placement
Classroom Connections
Family Connections
Unique Needs
School/Community Connections
Exit Transitions

PROFESSIONAL LEARNING—PLANNING FOR IMPLEMENTATION

1. After the specific action steps have been determined and roles are assigned, begin determining the necessary professional learning that will need to take place to support the steps of the plan.
2. Determine specific groups of people who will need to be trained on understanding and implementing the Mobility Action Plan. Be sure to include both certified and classified staff members.
3. Depending upon the size of the district, begin developing specific schedules for training, including the point person or people who will conduct the training itself.
4. Professional learning should be differentiated to meet the needs of elementary, middle, and high schools. You may want to consider training people by grade levels, by multidisciplinary teams, or by departments.
5. Consider how you might utilize technology to deploy training on a large scale if you are in a district where size can be a barrier for including all staff members.

IMPLEMENTATION—PUTTING THE PLAN INTO ACTION

1. Once the plan has been formed and training has been completed, it is time to begin putting things into practice. Ideally, this can happen at the beginning of the year. If that is not possible, begin with the very next students and families who walk through the door.
2. Establish regular checkpoints to determine the effectiveness of the plan, making adjustments where necessary over time. Put the checkpoints on the calendar rather than waiting to schedule at a later time. This is one of the main barriers to maintaining effective practices.
3. Designate the contact person responsible for making sure the plan is reviewed regularly and who will hold staff members accountable for following the established practices. This may be the principal, a counselor, or another staff member willing to take on the role. When choosing the person for this role, focus on specific strengths to determine a good fit. Is the person organized? Are deadlines a priority? Are issues addressed right away in order to take corrective action?
4. Determine the feedback mechanisms that will be used to measure the effectiveness of the steps within the action plan. Will you follow up with personal phone calls, conduct meaningful surveys, or invite parents in as a focus group? How will you get information

from students? Whatever you use to gather information, make it concise and clearly connected to the action plan steps.

5. Consider these sample questions:

   Poor question: Did you feel welcomed at our school?
   Better question: Did someone in the office greet you when you entered our school?

6. As you gather feedback throughout the year, make necessary changes or additions to the Mobility Action Plan. As you look to the following school year, determine when you will provide training for both new and existing staff members. The training that is provided can be enriched over time to include success stories and specific ways your school has seen a positive impact on students and school climate.

7. Plan the work and work the plan. Over time, the practices will be integrated into the fabric of the school, and you will make a significant difference in the lives of students.

Bibliography

Addressing the causes and consequences of high student mobility: The role of school systems and communities. (2002). A forum brief—American Youth Policy Forum.

Archived information: Schoolwide Programs—Title I, Part A, Policy Guidance. U.S. Department of Education. (1996). Electronic preference formats recommended by the American Psychological Association. Retrieved March 30, 2005 from http://www.ed.gov/legislation/ESEA/Title_I/swpguid1.html, 3.

Bennett, J. M. (Ed.). (1998). *Transition shock: Putting culture shock in perspective.* Yarmouth, ME: Intercultural Press.

Center for Mental Health in Schools at UCLA. (2007). *Welcoming and involving new students and families.* Los Angeles, CA: Author.

Clark, S. (2001, March/April). Managing mobility. Catalyst for Cleveland schools. Retrieved from http://www.catalyst-cleveland.org/04-01/0401standards.htm

Creswell, J. (2005). *Educational research: Planning, conducting, and evaluating quantitative and qualitative research.* 2nd ed. Upper Saddle River, NJ: Merrill/Prentice Hall.

Deady, F. X. (1997). The effect of school transfers due to mobility on students' self-concepts and academic performance. Doctoral dissertation, Temple University, Philadelphia, PA.

DiGiorgi, L. (2001). Tapestry weaving: How one school's Title I Schoolwide Program provided the hidden warp of school reform. Master's thesis, Pacific Lutheran University, Tacoma, WA.

"Easing the impact of student mobility: Welcoming and social support." (1997). Addressing barriers to learning. UCLA *School Mental Health Project Newsletter* 2 (4).

Fisher, T. A., L. Matthews, M. E. Stafford, K. Nakagawa, & K. Durante. (2002). School personnel's perceptions of effective programs for working with mobile students and families. *The Elementary School Journal* 102 (4): 317–333.

Fowler-Finn, T. (2001). Student stability vs. mobility—Factors that contribute to achievement gaps. *School Administrator.*

Franke, T. M., J. A. Iskin, & M. T. Parra. (2003). A pervasive school culture for the betterment of student outcomes: One school's approach to student mobility. *The Journal of Negro Education* 72 (1): 150–157.

Franke, T. M., & C. Hartman. (Eds.). (2003). Student mobility: How some children get left behind. *The Journal of Negro Education* 72 (1): 147–169.

Garcia, M. E. P. (1999). Level of involvement of Title I parents in a south Texas school district. Doctoral dissertation, Texas A&M University-Kingsville, Kingsville, TX.

Hull, Dana. "Turnover in the classroom: Constant churn of student transfers linked to lower test scores, teacher problems." *San Jose Mercury News,* April 25, 2005. Retrieved from http://www.mercurynews.com

Jennings, J. F. (Jack). (2000). Title I: Its legislative history and its promise. *Phi Delta Kappan* 81 (7): 516–522.

Kirst, Michael W. (1987). The federal role and Chapter I: Rethinking some basic assumptions. *Federal Aid,* 97–115.

Lash, A. A., & S. L. Kirkpatrick. (1990). A classroom perspective on student mobility. *The Elementary School Journal* 91 (2): 177–191.

Lash, A. A., & S. L. Kirkpatrick. (1994). Interrupted lessons: Teacher views of transfer student education. *American Education Research Journal* 31 (4): 813–843.

Lewis, A. (1996). Tinkering with Title I. *Phi Delta Kappan* 77 (10): 653–654.

Lunon, J. K. (1986). Migrant student record transfer system: What is it and who uses it? ERIC Digest: CRESS. Las Cruces, NM: New Mexico State University, ERIC Clearinghouse on Rural Education and Small Schools.

Maslow, A. (1970). *Motivation and personality* , 2nd ed. New York: Harper & Row.

Mense, E. G. (2004). A study to investigate the relationship between federal Title I program design and Title I student performance. Doctoral dissertation, Saint Louis University, St. Louis, MO.

New directions: Federal education policy in the twenty-first century. (March 1999). Published by the Thomas B. Fordham Foundation in cooperation with the Manhattan Institute for Policy Research.

No Child Left Behind Act of 2001, Title I, part C, sec.1309 (2).

Paik, S., & R. Phillips. (2002). Student mobility in rural communities: What are the implications for student achievement? North Central Regional Educational Laboratory: Learning Point Associates. Retrieved from http://www.ncrel.org

Payne, R. (2001). *A framework for understanding poverty.* Highland, TX: aha! Process, Inc.

Popp, P. A. (2004). Reading on the go! Students who are highly mobile and reading instruction. Prepared for the National Center for Homeless Education.

Popp, P. A., J. H. Stronge, & J. L. Hindman. (2003). Students on the move: Reaching and teaching highly mobile children and youth. National Center for Homeless Education at SERVE and ERIC Clearinghouse on Urban Education.

Puma, M. J. (1999). The "Prospects" study of educational growth and opportunity: Implications for policy and practice. Paper presented at the annual meeting of the American Educational Research Association, Montreal, Quebec, Canada. ERIC Document Reproduction Service No. ED 429.355.

Rhodes, V. L. (2005). Kids on the move: The effects of student mobility on NCLB school accountability ratings. *Perspectives* 3 (3). University of Pennsylvania Graduate School of Education.

Rumberger, R. (2003). *Student mobility and academic achievement.* Champaign, IL: ERIC Digest.

Salant, P., & A. Dillman. (1994). *How to conduct your own survey.* New York: John Wiley & Sons, Inc.

Salley, V. (2004). *Moving on: Student mobility and affordable housing.* Louisville, KY: Metropolitan Housing Coalition.

Sanderson, D. (2003). Veteran teachers' perspectives on student mobility. *Essays in Education* 4. Retrieved July 30, 2006, from http://www.usca.edu/essays/vol4winter2003.html

Students move: Supporting students who change schools. (2004, February). A report to the Commonwealth Department of Education, Science and Training.

U.S. General Accounting Office. (1992). Remedial education: Modifying Chapter I formula would target more funds to those most in need. Washington, DC.

Weckstein, P. (2003). "Accountability and student mobility under Title I of the No Child Left Behind Act." Student mobility: How some children get left behind. *The Journal of Negro Education* 72 (1): 117–125.

Westbrooks, H. M. (1996). Principals' perceptions of transient adolescents in rural middle schools. Doctoral dissertation, Southern Illinois University, Carbondale, IL. pp. 270–271.

Wong, K., & S. Meyer. (1998). Title I Schoolwide Programs: A synthesis of findings from recent evaluation. *Educational Evaluation and Policy Analysis* 20 (2): 115–136.

Made in the USA
San Bernardino, CA
17 January 2018